Nothing trumps overflow from our private time with the Lord. Dr Richard Blackaby is a masterful expositor of God's word. The outworking of the inworking of Christ in Richard's life will inspire and influence your walk with our Heavenly Father.

— JOHNNY HUNT, Senior Pastor, FBC, Woodstock, GA

Whether serving as a senior pastor, seminary president or president of Blackaby Ministries International, Richard Blackaby is a visible demonstration of what it means to be *Living Out of the Overflow*. His new book of the same title is one that should bless those who may be living minimally, yet long to live in God's abundance.

— ANNE GRAHAM LOTZ, President and Founder of AnGeL Ministries

In true Richard Blackaby fashion, *Living Out of the Overflow*, is yet another example of his extraordinary gift of uncovering profound and timely insights from God's Word. Richard's exceptional examination of Scripture's chronicling of its heroes will be a source of encouragement and inspiration for the days when our faith is flagging and our passion is dwindling. I would highly recommend passing this book along to anyone who needs a fresh and personal touch of spiritual vitality from his or her heavenly Father.

— JEFF CHRISTOPHERSON, VP Send Network (NAMB). Author, *Kingdom Matrix: Designing a Church for the Kingdom of God,* and *Kingdom First: Starting Churches that Shape Movements.*

God has gifted Richard with profound insights into His word and an unusual ability to communicate those truths in a manner that elicits maximum impact upon an audience. I have spoken with Richard around the world and the results have always been the same. This book represents Richard at his Bible-teaching best.

— HENRY BLACKABY, author of *Experiencing God*

Through his speaking and writing, Dr. Richard Blackaby has been a wonderful encouragement to Georgia Baptists. In this marvelous book, Richard will bless you as he has blessed us through enlightening revelation of truths from God's Word that will encourage, inspire and energize you and your ministry. I know of no family that has been more effective at discipling us out of the overflow of God's abundance than the Blackabys. This book is another Blackaby treasure.

— DR. J. ROBERT WHITE, Executive Director, Georgia Baptist Mission Board

...compelling, challenging, inspiring and tremendously encouraging. This book is an amazingly in-depth look at two spiritual giants ~ Moses and Elijah ~ whose life experiences were so long ago, yet, are so relevant for spiritual leaders today. Though easy and fun to read, it will challenge your heart and clarify biblical leadership. Before a pastor makes the next big decision in his life and/or ministry, this is a must read. Likewise, before a spiritual leader takes on the next responsibility, read this book. The profound biblical lessons carefully explained will make it another Blackaby treasure passed on for generations to come.

— JOHNNY RUMBOUGH, Director of Missions, Lexington Baptist Association, South Carolina

Richard Blackaby has managed once again to take a Bible story that is fairly common to me and look at it from an entirely different angle and perspective. Not only did I gain fresh new insight into this incredible story about Elijah, I also was encouraged and grateful for the practical application to my own life personally. This book will help leaders live through those roller coaster rides of life that sometimes can be exhilarating, but also can drive us into despair. If you've ever experienced those ups and downs of ministry or business you need to read this book.

— RICK BOXX, Founder and CEO, Integrity Resource

The Lord spoke as I read this book --Revival will not come until God's servants are willing to pray in the wilderness and our vital encounter with the Holy God overflows out into our people and communities. A must read for desperate times. Thank you, Richard Blackaby, for showing us God's Word, God's Way.

   — DR. STUART D. BROBERG, The Church of the Covenant, (Presbyterian) Washington, Pennsylvania

Every leader has experienced seasons of attempting to lead when the well runs dry. This book will change those seasons of your life forever. In this book, Richard with great compassion and detail describes how leaders can discover victory even in life's driest seasons. People often use the phrase "this is a life-changing book" -but I can attest this truly is a life-changing book. It is a book every leader must read and read often.

   — MARK CLIFTON, Senior Director of Church Replanting (NAMB)

Dr. Richard Blackaby is a marvelous teacher and insightful Christian writer and theologian. His teachings have transformed the lives of dozens of CEOs of major global companies over the last decade. In their dynamic, stressful, and high-paced positions of leadership, most, if not all, of these CEOs often live in a barren and dry land where it seems there is no water. Living out of the abundance and overflow of God through an intimate daily walk with Jesus has been their place of refuge, strength, and renewal. Heavenly provision has been the feedstock for effective Christ-centered leadership at the highest levels in our land.

   —RICK LYTLE, CEO, CEO Forum

LIVING OUT OF THE OVERFLOW

SERVING OUT OF YOUR INTIMACY WITH GOD

Richard Blackaby

Blackaby Ministries International

Jonesboro, Georgia

LIVING OUT OF THE OVERFLOW: SERVING OUT OF YOUR
INTIMACY WITH GOD
PUBLISHED BY BLACKABY MINISTRIES INTERNATIONAL
P.O. Box 1035
Jonesboro, GA 30237
www.blackaby.org

ISBN 978-0-692-84237-9

Publisher's Cataloging-in-Publication data

Names: Blackaby, Richard, 1961-, author.
Title: Living out of the overflow : serving out of your intimacy with God / Richard Blackaby.
Description: Includes bibliographical references | Jonesboro, GA: Blackaby Ministries International, 2017.
Identifiers: ISBN 978-0-692-84237-9 | LCCN 2017934002
Subjects: LCSH Christian life. | Spiritual life--Christianity. | God (Christianity)--Knowableness. | BISAC RELIGION / Christian Life / General
Classification: LCC BV4501.3 .B534 2017 | DDC 248.4--dc23

Printed in the United States of America
2017 — 3rd ed

Contents

Forward ....*ix*

Preface ....*xiii*

Introduction ....*xvii*

Section One: Elijah: Preparing for Mount Carmel 1

   1. Faithful in a Difficult Task 5

   2. Faithful in a Wilderness 17

   3. Faithful in Humble Circumstances..........................29

   4. Trusting God for a Miracle 43

Section Two: Elijah: Restored at Mount Sinai 59

   5. A Vulnerable Moment 63

   6. Withdrawing to God 81

   7. Returning to the Heights 97

   8. Restored for Service 109

   9. On Mission with God 121

Section Three: Moses: Pursuing God's Vision 137

   10. Holding on to a Dream 141

   11. Enemies of the Dream 151

   12. Facing Opposition 165

   13. God's Answer 175

   14. Rebels 187

   15. Hallowed 197

Conclusion 207

About the Author 213

FOREWORD

The Spirit-filled life is simple enough for a child to understand, yet often shrouded in mystery and confusion for even the most seasoned Christian. Misunderstanding, poor exegesis, and incorrect teaching on the Holy Spirit's place and purpose have left the church crippled and inept, thirsting for much more when the Living Water has already been poured out in and through them.

The Apostle Paul often exhorted the churches regarding the Spirit's power and provision.

*But I say, **walk by the Spirit,** and you will not gratify the desires of the flesh. For the desires of the flesh are against the Spirit, and the desires of the Spirit are against the flesh, for these are opposed to each other, to keep you from doing the things you want to do. . . . And those who belong to Christ Jesus have crucified the flesh with its passions and desires. If we **live by the Spirit,** let us also **keep in step with the Spirit.*** (Galatians 5:16, 17, 24, 25)

*Therefore do not be foolish, but understand what the will of the Lord is. And do not get drunk with wine, for that is debauchery, but **be filled with the Spirit,** addressing one another in psalms and hymns and spiritual songs, singing and making melody to the Lord with your heart, giving thanks* *always and for everything to God the Father in the name of our Lord Jesus Christ, submitting to one another out of reverence for Christ.* (Ephesians 5:17-21)

Taking their cues from Paul, theologians, authors, and laymen alike have implored believers throughout history in their pursuit of the Spirit-filled life.

"The motive for being filled with the Spirit is not my own personal enjoyment, but divine employment so that God can use my life through which to bless others. . . . You use me as a riverbed and let the Spirit of God flow through me. I think that is the simple way that Jesus intended us to come into the fullness of the Spirit." – Ron Dunn

"To be filled with the Spirit is to have the Spirit fulfilling in us all that God intended him to do when he placed him there." – Lewis Sperry Chafer

"God commands us to be filled with the Spirit, and if we are not filled it is because we are living beneath our privileges." – D. L. Moody

"The Spirit-filled life is not a special, deluxe edition of Christianity. It is part and parcel of the total plan of God for his people." – A. W. Tozer

"The best evidence of being truly filled with the Spirit is that one so filled 'continues daily.' The glory shows up in the grind! As important as the grandeur of getting started is the grace of going on!" – Vance Havner

We've received valuable wisdom, insight, and teaching throughout the ages. God has clearly spoken in His Word, and He has not stuttered. So why another book on what Christian living is supposed to look like? Why read this one about living the victorious Christian life? Because we forget and we need reminding. Because we lose focus and become attracted to the temporary pleasures of this world, and we need fresh vision. Because if we don't walk in victory and in all Christ has accomplished for us on the cross, then we're way off track and need to return to the basics.

In his book *Living Out of the Overflow*, my friend Richard Blackaby takes a fresh look at living the victorious Christian life through the lives of Elijah and Moses. This in depth journey through the lives of these men doesn't just highlight their moments of triumph. Rather, Richard details their pits of despair, frustration, defeat, disappointment, unbelief, and disobedience as well. How did these two respond in the face of adversity?

How did they walk with God even in times of difficulty and discouragement? And what can we learn from their example when we face similar roadblocks in our own lives? Their intimacy with the Father gave them a firm footing when all else was uncertain.

On the shelves of my study are numerous books with the name Blackaby on the cover. Why? Because through the years I've found that name, whether Henry or one of his sons, is a name that I can trust. I can trust the content of the book to be sound theologically. I can trust the author to be a living witness of the truths he puts in print. I can trust that the methods and writings have been proven and worked out in real life, not just while sitting at a computer.

Richard Blackaby is a name you can trust. His insights rise above denominations, opinions, or personal preferences. He stays true to the Word and the accurate application of Scripture. This newest book is no different. If you've ever wondered if there's "something more" beyond the daily grind or if you've ever found yourself dry and barren and thirsting for abundant living, find solace in the Scripture interpreted and applied throughout these pages. Take heart in knowing that for thousands of years our extraordinary God has taken great delight in doing extraordinary things through very ordinary people. Isn't it time you lived out of the overflow?

Michael Catt
Senior Pastor,
Sherwood Baptist Church, Albany, GA

PREFACE

Few things (other than grandchildren) give me as much joy as 1) teaching the Bible and 2) encouraging church leaders. This book allows me to do both!

For many years I have had the privilege of traveling around the world and speaking to gatherings of church leaders. While I have taught a wide array of topics, I repeatedly return to a handful of chapters in the Bible. These chapters are heavy-laden with rich truths for Christians and church leaders. Every time I teach from these passages, I receive an overwhelmingly positive response.

Last year I spoke from some of my favorite leadership passages in the Bible. During the breaks, people kept asking me, "Is this in a book somewhere?" Others exclaimed, "If this were in print, I'd give a copy to every leader I work with." I began to sense God leading me to publish these encouraging truths so people around the world could benefit from them.

This book is unlike anything I have written before. It delves deeply into just three chapters of the Bible. But what amazing chapters they are! It also looks at only two primary characters. But again, they are spiritual giants who inevitably inspire those who encounter them. So I invite you to join me on an exhilarating journey through three passages that will undoubtedly encourage you. While I have attempted to write this material to the best of my ability, the amazing truths you encounter are what will impact you most. I hope, not that you will like this book, but that it will forever change you!

I'd like to offer special thanks to a handful of people who made this book what it is. First, thanks to my dad, Henry Blackaby, who gave me a love for God's word and delight in encouraging church leaders. My dad is a spiritual giant who taught me to draw near to any spiritual giant in the vicinity, whether living or on the pages of Scripture or history.

Thanks to my wife, Lisa, who has graciously and sacrificially supported my call to travel the world sharing these truths with people who desperately need them. I appreciate her willingness to hold the fort upstairs in our house so I could slip downstairs to my study to write down another thought God revealed to me through His word.

Thanks to my daughter, Carrie Blackaby Camp, who is an extremely talented writer. She painstakingly transformed a manuscript that made perfect sense to me into a book that would be intelligible to readers as well! Thanks to my daughter-in-law Sarah Emily Blackaby who designed the cover and took care of all manner of technical issues on my behalf. Thanks also to Rick Fisher, the Administrative Vice President of Blackaby Ministries International, who gave invaluable assistance to this project. Thanks also to Steve Parsons for his technological expertise. Finally, thanks to my oldest son, Mike Blackaby, as well as my friend Bob Payne, and brother-in-law Wendell Webb, who offered valuable insights as I was shaping this manuscript.

A special thanks to Don and Ruthie Jacobsen who generously made their beautiful home in the north Georgia mountains available to me so I could compose a book that could provide other people a "mountain top" experience. Thanks also to Paul Spence who kindly made his townhouse at the beach available when I was doing the final edits.

If you are someone who currently needs encouragement or inspiration, read this book carefully, prayerfully, and alertly. I am convinced the truths embedded in the following pages can radically transform your life. I know this to be true because they have changed me.

Richard Blackaby
President, Blackaby Ministries International

INTRODUCTION

There are sacred moments in Jesus' life that are profoundly mysterious. Scripture offers us glimpses of them, but our meager experience and knowledge prevent us from grasping their magnitude.

Such was the case on the Mount of Transfiguration. Jesus approached His ministry's climax. Calvary loomed. The powers of darkness schemed. His disciples slept.

We cannot comprehend the unimaginable horror that awaited the sinless Son of God. The unfathomable weight of humanity's sins would be fully laid upon Him. Sinister, dark forces bitterly resolved to destroy Jesus and thwart God's purposes. The fate of every person throughout history hung in the balance. If Jesus made a mistake, lost heart, or was deceived, all was lost. There was no margin for error. There was no second chance.

God the Father summoned His Son to the Mount of Transfiguration. From that holy peak, the Father and Son looked toward the cross. Jesus' crucifixion and subsequent resurrection would be the culmination of the sacred plans the Father drafted before time began.

During those hallowed moments, Jesus' divinity burst forth from His human frame. His face shone like the sun. His clothes glowed brilliantly. Centuries earlier when Moses met with God, Moses' face glowed as it reflected God's glory (Ex. 34:29-35). But this was no secondary glory. Here, for a fleeting moment, the disciples witnessed the breathtaking majesty of the Son of God overflowing the banks of His mortal flesh.

Later, when the Roman soldiers beat and crucified Jesus, His glory was once again concealed. Yet it was this same glorious Christ who they brutally nailed to a cruel cross. It was this face they would scornfully spit upon.

Atop the mountain, the Father prepared His Son for the greatest achievement in human history. Peter, James, and John, presumably the disciples closest to Him, were also present. But added to that enclave were two unusual guests: Moses and Elijah. Extraordinary men summoned for a magnificent undertaking.

If your son faced imminent execution, who would you want to visit him in his final hours? The heavenly Father chose Moses and Elijah. This decision demonstrates how crucial the Father viewed this consultation. Not only did He attend it Himself, He summoned two people from the dead! Since God had complete access to the grave, He could have recalled anyone from history. Imagine if Adam had come to encourage the second Adam in His work to restore what he had lost (Rom. 5:19). David might have attended to inspire Jesus to stand firm in the face of His enemies. Abraham, the father of the faithful and the friend of God, surely could have extolled Jesus to keep the faith (James 2:23). Job could have encouraged Jesus to persevere in the midst of suffering. God might have appointed any number of people to undergird His Son as He prepared to undertake history's greatest task. Therefore, it is significant to note which two people God chose to invite.

Moses represented the Law while Elijah symbolized the prophets. Certainly Moses was the greatest of Israel's lawgivers and Elijah the mightiest of Israel's prophets. Moses may have discussed how Jesus' death on the cross would at last fulfill the demand for righteousness required by the law. Elijah may have reviewed how Jesus' life fulfilled numerous predictions by the prophets throughout the ages. But for anyone who has experienced and observed the workings of the Lord, it is clear that God has a multiplicity of reasons for His actions. We cannot help but wonder if God summoned Moses and Elijah not only for what they represented, but also for who they were. Perhaps their personal experiences qualified them to offer practical encouragement to the Messiah at such a crucial moment.

Moses and Elijah had much in common. For example, mountains played a crucial role in their lives. Moses and Elijah were the only two people to meet with God personally on Mount Sinai. God called Moses into service at Mount Horeb. Elijah's call was renewed at that mount. Likewise, Jesus' life was punctuated by mountains such as Olives, Moriah, Transfiguration, and Calvary.

Moses and Elijah boldly stood in the gap for their nation. Moses pleaded with God, *"Now if You would only forgive their sin. But if not, please erase me from the book You have written"* (Ex. 32:32). Likewise, when Israel's apostasy reached its zenith, Elijah stood before his nation and cried out to God, *"Answer me, Lord! Answer me so the people will know that You, Yahweh, are God and that You have turned their hearts back"* (1

Kings 18:37). Jesus, dying on the cross for the sins of humanity, prayed, *"Father, forgive them, because they do not know what they are doing"* (Luke 23:34).

Evil government authorities plotted against and pursued both Moses and Elijah. Pharaoh sought Moses' life. Jezebel schemed to kill Elijah. Both men witnessed God's miraculous power. Both men grew discouraged when their ministries became difficult. Both men pleaded with God to allow them to quit in the face of continual opposition. Finally, both men ended their life in a mysterious manner. God Himself buried Moses on Mount Nebo (Deut. 34:5-6). Satan and the archangel Michael fought over his corpse (Jude 9). A fiery chariot swept up Elijah and transported him to heaven (2 Kings 2:11).

Many of these two men's experiences were similar to those of Jesus. They learned much over the course of their illustrious lives. Now the Father asked them to walk with His Son as He prepared for the greatest challenge of His life.

If the heavenly Father chose to bring Moses and Elijah alongside His beloved Son to encourage Him, might they also bring hope, insight, and perspective to you as well? If you have been given a task that seems beyond your abilities or if you have grown weary in well doing, you will identify with these men. If critics and naysayers are mercilessly hounding you, these men know what you are going through. If you long for God to use your ordinary life to impact your nation, these men did too. If you are in a spiritual wilderness, these men have something to offer you.

I wrote this book to encourage the many Christians who are striving to faithfully serve their Lord in the midst of difficulty and opposition. There are numerous Christians today who are suffering through spiritual "dry" periods. Christian leaders are experiencing burnout in alarming numbers. This despite the fact that Jesus placed a fountain of living water within them (John 4:14).

Many Christians' souls have become barren and parched due to life's trials and burdens. Pastors have become so frustrated by how people behaved that their own hearts grew hardened and bitter. Long-time Christians find that, despite years of attending church services, their devotional life has grown stale and lifeless. Others grow dissatisfied with their walk with God and try to supplement it with worldly philosophies, materialism, self-help therapies, and even immorality. The great irony is that Christians have living water available within them, yet they keep looking for nourishment from external sources that cannot satisfy. God would say to us, as He did to the people of Jeremiah's time: *"For My people have committed a double evil: They have abandoned Me, the fountain of living water, and dug cisterns for themselves, cracked cisterns that cannot hold water"* (Jer. 2:13).

In the following pages I want to share a treasure trove of biblical truths that can help you experience living water each day as you abide in Christ. I invite you to walk alongside Moses and Elijah to see how they ultimately learned how to live and lead out of the overflow of their personal walk with God, regardless of their circumstances. I have shared these truths with audiences around the world, and they have never failed to refresh those who received them.

I pray that, as you read these pages, you will not only find spiritual refreshing and nourishment, but you will be empowered to undertake God's assignment for you. I pray that, as you are reminded of what the Holy Spirit did in the lives of those who went before you, you will be inspired to seek the Spirit-filled life for yourself as well. God's provision is as available to you today as it was for Gideon, Moses, David, Peter, Mary, and Paul. Jesus declares today as He did 2000 years ago: *"If anyone is thirsty, he should come to Me and drink! The one who believes in Me, as the Scripture has said, will have streams of living water flow from deep within him"* (John 7:37-38). God doesn't just want you to survive. He wants you to live and minister out of the overflow of His abundance.

Elijah: Preparing for Mount Carmel

INTRODUCTION

Elijah is one of the grandest figures in the Bible. He arrived suddenly and departed spectacularly. He appeared invincible at certain moments and painfully vulnerable at others. He was a man of mystery. He soared above the ordinary, yet Scripture assures us he was just as limited by his humanity as we are (James 5:17). He performed some of history's greatest miracles, yet found comfort in the mundane. Though he failed to bring lasting revival to his nation, he left a successor with a double portion of his spirit (2 Kings 2:9-10). At the close of the Old Testament, the prophet Malachi foresaw Elijah's return as preparatory to the Messiah's coming (Mal. 4:5). Then, as the world's Savior prepared for His climactic rendezvous at Golgotha, Elijah, accompanied by Moses, shared a uniquely glorious moment with Him on a sacred mount (Matt. 17:1-3).

Though he became renowned for spectacular feats, Elijah may be best remembered for his epic confrontation on Mount Carmel. There, the solitary prophet faced 450 prophets of Baal and 400 prophets of Asherah. That dramatic encounter captivates our imaginations, for it encapsulates the age-old struggle between good and evil. Queen Jezebel propelled her evil husband Ahab to abominable depths until he sanctioned the widespread arrest and murder of God's prophets (1 Kings 18:4; 21:25). There was no policy of toleration. God's servants were to be annihilated.

Then, after the three-and-a-half-year drought Elijah pronounced, history witnessed one of the greatest tests of strength ever undertaken (James 5:17). Atop Mount Carmel, 850 false prophets faced one solitary man of God. The idolatrous clerics cried out to their idol all day, loudly proclaiming their devotion. Then as evening dawned, Elijah took center stage. His life hung in the balance. He knew full well that if God did not answer decisively and quickly, he would never leave the mountain alive. He prayed a simple, faithful, confident prayer. And fire fell. Oh that every servant of God would experience that exhilarating moment when they cry out to God and He answers with fire! God chose to honor His servant before a watching nation that day. The people's response was to shout, *"Yahweh, He is God!"* (1 Kings 18:39). It was a high water mark for the nation that echoes through the centuries to our day.

We live in an age much like Elijah's. Many people have chosen to forsake the true God to pursue idols that promise riches and pleasure without demanding holy living. The government increasingly applies pressure on the Church to compromise its values and standards. Evil forces relentlessly strive to exclude God's people from having any voice in national affairs. Many of God's servants have grown silent or gone into hiding. We live in an age that desperately needs another Elijah.

Our society urgently requires men and women who will fearlessly take a stand for God. We need people who walk so closely with God that the moment they pray, heavenly fire descends. The Church is searching for people who have the ear of God when they pray and the hand of God when they act. This is not a time for casual, powerless, fence-sitting ministry. We desperately require modern-day Elijahs.

Were it easy to become a weather-altering, nation-rattling, king-frightening, darkness-dispelling, servant of God, volunteers would abound. But the path Elijah took to Mount Carmel was as circuitous as it was hazardous.

When God intends to accomplish a great work through His servants, He always prepares them. Not everyone is willing to remain in God's school of faith and prayer until God's work is complete. Elijah did, and we continue to read his story three millennia later.

The story of Elijah on Mount Carmel is widely known, so we will not devote much time discussing it in this volume. What people are less familiar with is what God did to prepare Elijah to be a catalyst for national revival. It is to that period in Elijah's life we now turn.

CHAPTER ONE

Faithful in a Difficult Task

1.ELIJAH'S QUALIFICATIONS

"Now Elijah the Tishbite, from the Gilead settlers, said to Ahab, 'As the Lord God of Israel lives, I stand before Him, and there will be no dew or rain during these years except by my command'" (1 Kings 17:1).

The greatest prophet of the Bible suddenly appears before the wickedest king of the age and yet we know almost nothing about him. Elijah's unexpected arrival reveals much about the One who dispatched him.

God certainly would have been justified in commissioning a spokesperson sooner. Ahab had acted wickedly throughout his reign. Ahab's father, Omri, had certainly qualified for a prophetic visit (1 Kings 16:21). Nevertheless, God waited until this particular moment to speak. God's timing is always perfect.

We are told that Elijah was a Tishbite, which presumably means he was from the village of Tishbe. We are also informed that he was from the people of Gilead. Yet the only Tishbe so far known to us is not in Gilead but twelve miles north of the Jabbok River in Naphtali. Perhaps he migrated from Naphtali to Gilead. Or perhaps his village in Gilead was so small that no trace of it remains today. Clearly Elijah's pedigree was inconsequential to his commissioning. Elijah mentioned none of his personal background to the king. The key to Elijah's influence was not what he had done in the past, but how he related to God in the present (Phil. 3:13). Where you are from clearly matters far less to God than where you are going.

The prophet duly announced his life message: *"As the Lord God of Israel lives . . ."* Every message Elijah preached highlighted this one fundamental truth. The true God is very much alive and ruling! Elijah not only preached this message, he lived it. You could not observe Elijah's life for long without concluding that Elijah served a living, active, powerful God. The evidence was too compelling to think otherwise.

Elijah submitted only one credential to the king. He declared: *"I stand before Him."* What more did he need to say? Can a divine spokesperson have a greater qualification than regularly abiding in God's presence? To stand before the almighty indicates you know His thoughts and intentions. Elijah's personal circumstances mattered not at all. He had come from the King's presence.

Today many of God's people complain that they are unqualified to serve the Lord. They have never been to seminary. They lack confidence in their Bible knowledge. They feel inadequate to speak publicly. They do not view themselves as leaders. Yet every believer has an equal opportunity to obtain Elijah's qualification. All may enter the holy of holies (Heb. 4:16).

Jesus said to His disciples: *"I do not call you slaves anymore, because a slave doesn't know what his master is doing. I have called you friends, because I have made known to you everything I have heard from My Father"* (John 15:15). What an awesome privilege! There is no greater preparation for God's service than to know His heart and intentions. Parents cannot know the future as they help their child choose a career, but they can enter God's throne room and discover what is on His heart for their child. Pastors may not be the most eloquent orator in their city, but they can enter the holy place to discover God's thoughts about their flock.

Don't confuse Bible study with spending conscious time in God's presence. Never assume that because you participate in Christian activities you are abiding in Christ. You may have uttered a prayer, but that does not mean you have heard what is on God's heart. The single greatest habit a Christian can cultivate is the practice of abiding in God's presence. Never underestimate the enormous influence you can wield when you know the heart of God.

2.ELIJAH'S AUDIENCE

God told Elijah to deliver one of the most difficult sermons ever assigned to a preacher. Though we may assume there were guards and attendants present when Elijah spoke, King Ahab dominated the small congregation. When God commissions people to speak on His behalf, He is not obligated to grant a favorable hearing. Often the message elicits rejection or even hostility. Nonetheless, Elijah had an unusually difficult task, for King Ahab was unprecedentedly wicked. Scripture describes him this way: *"Ahab did more to provoke the Lord God of Israel than all the kings of Israel who were before him"* (1 Kings 16:33). The king's conduct made God angry! Sadly, he would not be the last government official to accomplish that feat. We should not be surprised. Scripture says this of Ahab's father: *"Omri did what was evil in the Lord's sight, he did more evil than all who were before him"* (1 Kings 16:25). Children tend to surpass their parents. God may have designed families to function this way. When we set the direction of our life toward righteousness, our children have the opportunity to stand on our spiritual shoulders to reach even greater heights of godliness. But when we pass down sin and character flaws to our offspring, they may well plummet to depths to which we ourselves would be ashamed to descend. One might have assumed that no king could exceed Omri in wickedness. Ahab proved such skeptics wrong.

God may have given Elijah previous assignments, but none are recorded. The first task noted in scripture is here, and it was exceedingly difficult. God commissioned Elijah to preach an extremely unpopular message to the man who had made God angrier than any of his predecessors. Ahab's wife had already butchered scores of God's prophets and Elijah may have assumed his sermon would earn him a trip to the gallows as well. Nevertheless, Elijah didn't complain about the unresponsive, resistant audience he was called to address. He knew he was simply a messenger. God wanted to send word to an evil, corrupt government leader, and He chose to do it through His servant Elijah.

Some messengers believe they have a right to choose their audience as well as their message. Not so with God's servants. Some speakers take personal offense if their presentation is not well received or they are not sufficiently thanked or remunerated for delivering it. Such should not be the case with God's spokesperson. The key to success for God's messenger is not the cleverness of their delivery, nor the responsiveness of their audience, but the fidelity with which they deliver the divine message.

3. ELIJAH'S MESSAGE

". . . there will be no dew or rain during these years
except by my command!" (1 Kings 17:1)

Some of history's most profound messages have
been remarkably brief. Abraham Lincoln's Gettysburg
Address lasted two minutes. A message need not be long
if it is inspired! Elijah wasted no time with a verbose
introduction. He did not soften the message's blow for
his listeners. Rather, he delivered the word God gave him
clearly, concisely, and courageously. Perhaps he feared
diluting his divine directive with his own utterances. He
knew the key to his success was not his words, but God's.

The prophet's message was pointed: There would be
no dew or rain. This startling proclamation announced
a direct test of strength between God and Baal. Baal was
associated with thunderstorms. His name derived from
a word meaning "lord, owner, or possessor." He was a
popular god among local farmers because he assured
adequate rainfall and successful harvests. God had
promised to provide for His people and to give them a
land flowing with milk and honey. But God was also a
holy deity with high standards for His people. Baal was
not. Baal promised people riches without requiring
righteousness. It was man-made religion to the extreme.

To make matters worse, King Ahab had married
Jezebel, daughter of Ethbaal, king of Sidon (1 Kings
16:31-33). Ethbaal, whose name meant, "With him is
Baal," promoted idol worship in that region (1 Kings

16:31). His daughter Jezebel, the personification of evil, used government power to hunt down and massacre God's prophets (1 Kings 18:4). The government was aggressively antagonistic to God and His purposes. It had intimidated God's prophets, mocked His standards, and ridiculed His commandments. God's response was decisive. There would be no rain. The people had forsaken the true God for a god of rain. So God struck at what was allegedly Baal's greatest strength—producing water. The people forsook God in their quest for prosperity, so God summarily removed their wealth from them. God's people can be certain of this: God is the avowed enemy of their idols. He is a jealous God (Ex. 20:5; Deut. 4:24). He despises anything in your life that takes His place. He will tolerate no rival to His rightful position as Lord.

This sermon was exceedingly unwelcome. Without rain, the Israelite farmers would have no crops. Without crops, they could pay no taxes nor provide food for the citizenry. Without taxes, Ahab could not fund his army or his royal lifestyle. A famine might lead to civil unrest. We can only imagine the alarm Ahab felt as he listened to Elijah that day.

God's servants are not afforded the luxury of choosing which messages they deliver. They do not have the right to tone them down to make them more palatable. While God's messengers should strive to be winsome and gracious, the primary measure of their success is how accurately they deliver the divine message. They do not measure their effectiveness by how appreciative their audience was of their sermon. Micaiah told the king the truth and his reward was imprisonment (1 Kings 22:1-28). Jeremiah preached faithfully for years, yet was continually rejected and imprisoned. Zechariah spoke truth to his generation and the king had him stoned to death (2 Chron. 24:20-22). At times, the only reward God's messengers receive for their effort is the palpable pleasure of their Master. Elijah preached faithfully and flawlessly, yet no gratitude was forthcoming from the people who most needed his message.

4. ELIJAH'S REWARD

"Then a revelation from the Lord came to him: 'Leave here, turn eastward, and hide yourself at the Wadi Cherith where it enters the Jordan'" (1 Kings 17:2-3).

Elijah had been assigned a difficult, hazardous task, and he had performed it flawlessly. You might think God would recompense His heroic servant magnificently. However, God's rewards rarely match our expectations.

Verse two begins with the word "then." *"Then a revelation from the Lord came to him"* (1 Kings 17:2). The word "then" identifies timing. It can reveal God's timing, when He chooses to speak, or people's timing, when they choose to respond. It is worth noting when God chose to communicate with Elijah. God spoke immediately after Elijah obeyed His previous instruction. At times we can experience silence from God. Our first response should be to take a spiritual inventory to ensure we have faithfully obeyed any earlier word we received from Him. God has no reason to grant us a fresh word if we have not yet obeyed His previous instruction.

When God speaks to Elijah, we expect Him to say, "Well done, good and faithful servant . . ." We assume God will provide the reliable prophet a respite. Perhaps Elijah will commence an itinerant speaking ministry where his newfound celebrity status as a court preacher brings him numerous invitations. Or, perhaps he will be offered a book contract where he can compile a compendium of his greatest sermons. At the very least, appreciative friends and colleagues should inundate him with cards and notes praising him for his courageous ministry in the nation's capital.

Instead, God told his faithful servant to withdraw and hide. This command strikes us as odd. Elijah will later call fire down on the heads of soldiers who are intent on arresting him (2 Kings 1:9-12). God certainly could have protected His messenger in a similar fashion on this occasion. But God did not. Instead He instructed Elijah to run from his enemies and hide by the Brook Cherith. Clearly not every confrontation is an appropriate occasion to engage in battle. Some pugilistic Christians assume they are failing their Lord if they do not arise and charge into battle every time God's honor is challenged. Avoiding conflict is viewed as cowardice. Yet in this instance we clearly see that not every assault demands a counterpunch. Many a youthful cleric has had his ministry come to an abrupt end because he wrongly assumed he must march into battle the first time an enemy appeared on the horizon. There are moments when battle is called for and other occasions when it is best to withdraw. If we will listen carefully to our Master, He will direct us to either advance, retreat, or stand our ground.

CONCLUSION

These first three verses present enormous contrasts. We meet a fearless prophet who boldly declared an unpopular message. Then we see him instructed to flee from his enemies. We find a servant of God faithfully carrying out a difficult assignment. Next we see him retreating into a wilderness. This sequence of events does not make sense to us. We assume that when people obey God's commands, He rewards them. When people faithfully carry out God's instructions, their life becomes better, not worse. Elijah did everything correctly and the result was that he became his nation's foremost fugitive. Even though Elijah was in the center of God's will, his life became more difficult. Elijah was unaware at that time, but though he was hurriedly making his way to the Brook Cherith, he was commencing a broader journey that would eventually lead to Mount Carmel. Were Elijah's story to end here, it would appear somehow tragic. Thankfully, when God directs your paths there is always another chapter to the story!

QUESTIONS TO CONSIDER

1. Have you spent more time worrying about your qualifications than you have invested drawing into God's presence?

2. How faithful have you been to obey, to the letter, God's assignments for you?

3. How accurately are you delivering God's message?

4. When you have obeyed God's assignment, has your life become easier or more difficult? How have you handled that?

5. Are you experiencing a period of divine silence? If so, why might that be?

CHAPTER TWO

Faithful in a Wilderness

"'Leave here, turn eastward, and hide yourself at the Wadi Cherith where it enters the Jordan. You are to drink from the wadi. I have commanded the ravens to provide for you there.' So he did what the Lord commanded. Elijah left and lived by the Wadi Cherith where it enters the Jordan. The ravens kept bringing him bread and meat in the morning and in the evening, and he drank from the wadi. After a while, the wadi dried up because there had been no rain in the land" (1 Kings 17:3-7).

1. ELIJAH'S NEXT ASSIGNMENT

Elijah obeyed everything God commanded. Nevertheless, his circumstances deteriorated drastically. He began his ministry in the royal court. He was subsequently assigned to a wilderness. Previously he spoke to kings. Afterward, his only companions were ravens. At first glance, Elijah appears to have been demoted.

The Wadi Cherith was an insignificant place. Bible scholars are uncertain of its exact location. It was lonely, quiet, and desolate. It certainly was not a post to which people were naturally drawn. But God stationed His premier prophet there.

We recoil from thoughts of inhabiting a wilderness because it instinctively strikes us as evil and undesirable. The entire adult population of Israel was consumed by God's wrath in the wilderness. The Israelites refused to trust God to give them the land of Canaan. God consigned the unbelieving Hebrews to the wilderness for 40 years until they perished. For the remainder of their lives, they dwelt in the shadow of God's promise, knowing they would never obtain it. The people of Elijah's day believed the wilderness was inhabited by demons and that evil forces did their most sinister work in such desolate, lonely environments. Throughout history, many people have faced their demons in the wilderness. When the Israelites found themselves in a wilderness, they had grave reason for concern.

We often have strong beliefs about how God should manage His kingdom. We assume that if we are faithful in small assignments, God will inevitably grant us larger ones. If we experience success with little, God will automatically assign us more. If we suffer for Him, God will reward us. This paradigm seems only fair to us. It strikes us as blatantly unjust for a pastor to faithfully serve a congregation and then to be assigned to a smaller church as a reward. Yet God feels no obligation to work according to our human reasoning or sense of fairness. God's handling of His most effective servant seems odd to us, but not to God. Elijah was absolutely faithful and his reward was a wilderness. Clearly God's ways are not identical to ours (Is. 55:8-9).

Not many of us will be consigned to a physical wilderness. But we could experience a spiritual, emotional, or career wasteland. Many ministers faithfully served their Lord in a local church. Eventually, ungodly congregants bent on power and control fired them. The wounded pastors were consigned to a wilderness. They used to be inundated with phone calls and messages. Now few people reach out to them. They used to have full calendars. Now they are unemployed. They were accustomed to the sound of voices and conversations. Now there is silence. Their future was once crowded with possibilities. Now it appears bleak and uncertain. It doesn't take long to transition from a noisy, busy life to quiet solitude in a wilderness.

When this transition occurs, sincere servants of God often experience anguish of soul as they ponder how they arrived at such a grim place. Did they make a mistake? Did they mishandle a situation? Are they failures as leaders? Should they have acted differently? Is God punishing them? We tend to assume that if we find ourselves in a wilderness, we must have done something wrong. The seeming unfairness of the situation only makes matters worse. The wicked king Ahab lounged in his opulent palace while Elijah eked out an existence at the mercy of ravens. Likewise, congregations have callously terminated their godly pastor. While the minister was bereft of salary, severance, and health insurance, the ungodly conspirators exerted control over the church. Ahab was the wicked person, yet he continued to live in luxurious comfort. Elijah was a righteous servant of God. Nevertheless, it was he who now resided in a wilderness.

God's servants often struggle in the wilderness. They are accustomed to others needing them, but now no one calls. They have habitually juggled frenetic schedules, but now they are idle. They are accustomed to assuming important roles and overcoming difficult challenges. Now they feel irrelevant. No one seems to value their skills and knowledge. Such a condition can be extremely unsettling. None of us are ever far from a wilderness. In fact, it might be closer to us than we think.

2. ELIJAH'S RESPONSE

Elijah was given an extremely difficult assignment. Preach an unwelcome sermon to an evil king. Elijah obeyed to the letter. However, rather than a reward or congratulations, God's next word was even more difficult. Go alone to a wilderness and trust notorious scavengers to feed you.

Although preaching a God-honoring sermon to Ahab invited disaster, at least it was a sermon. Elijah, after all, was the foremost orator of his day. But then God told him to leave his pulpit and relocate to a place where he had no audience.

Two issues seem peculiar at this point. First, obedience to God's command has seemingly made Elijah's life more difficult. He left his field of experience and giftedness as a preacher and was consigned to a place of loneliness and irrelevance. He had nothing to offer the wilderness. His presence made no difference. None of the wilderness creatures needed his leadership. Second, God seemed to be misusing a reliable prophet. Imagine being God and having Elijah at your disposal. He was the prophet of fire. He preached fearlessly. We might assume that God would commission him to preach on the steps of the capital or on Main Street, calling people to repent in the manner of Jonah in Nineveh. Had Elijah taken an inventory of his ministry gifts, he may well have assumed the best means of leveraging his skills was in the midst of large crowds and society's elite. But God had a different plan. God sent His finest preacher into a wilderness where no sermons were required. God gave no indication of how long Elijah's hiatus would last. God simply said go.

Notice Elijah's response. *"So he did what the Lord commanded. Elijah left and lived by the Wadi Cherith where it enters the Jordan"* (1 Kings 17:5). The English word "so" has only two letters, but people's destiny hinges on it. The Bible often reports how God revealed

His will to someone. Beside each divine conversation you could place a "so." So Abraham left his home and went to the land God showed him. So Moses argued with God. So Jonah fled in the opposite direction. So the Rich Young Ruler went away sad. So James and John immediately got out of their boat and followed Jesus. There is a "so" beside every word God speaks. If we respond in faith, our future unfolds in one manner. If we refuse to believe what God said, our future follows an entirely different course. Our life is filled with a series of "so's" that determines what our life becomes and what it accomplishes.

God never intended for His commands to be confusing. It is we who complicate matters. *"So he did what the Lord commanded"* (1 Kings 17:5). His routine, straightforward obedience made Elijah the greatest prophet of the Old Testament. God is under no obligation to justify His commands. His ways are not required to make sense to us. God's servants understand that they do not deserve any assignment from God, let alone one of prominence or comfort. For God to assign us to even the most obscure, difficult post on earth is an undeserved honor. Elijah recognized that he merited no heavenly reward for doing what his Creator commanded. He had no right to complain about his treatment or working conditions. Told to leave his prominent ministry and relocate to a place of obscurity, Elijah promptly arose and went.

3. THE NATURE OF A WILDERNESS

The question remains: why would God send his most effective servant into a wilderness? Of course, this query assumes a wilderness is an unwelcome place. The truth is that God does some of His best work in solitude. The nature of a wilderness makes it conducive for producing certain fruit in our life.

The wilderness is quiet. Devoid of chatter, hearing the Spirit's still small voice becomes much easier. Without the constant buzz of activity, we have time to reflect and think deeply. We have space to pray in a wilderness. In such a venue, God does not need to raise His voice. Relieved of responsibilities for others, we have time to focus on God and what He wants to do in us. No longer distracted with *doing*, we can focus on *being*.

Consider Jesus' example. He began His public ministry by being baptized to *"fulfill all righteousness"* (Matt. 3:15). The Father was so pleased with His Son's righteous obedience He audibly declared, *"This is My beloved Son. I take delight in Him!"* (Matt. 3:17). Imagine being so pleasing to your heavenly Father that He chose to let everyone around you know how proud He was of you. What might you expect the Father to do next? The subsequent verse declares: *"Then Jesus was led up by the Spirit into the wilderness . . ."* (Matt. 4:1). Why would the Father consign a perfectly obedient Son to solitude in a wilderness? Because certain work is accomplished best in that environment.

Our lives are typically filled with noise and commotion. We may occasionally complain that we need to slow down and spend more time with God, but we seldom do. Occasionally God's response is to lead us into a wilderness. God will do whatever is necessary to help us become like Christ. If a wilderness experience was necessary for Jesus, don't assume you have no need of one yourself.

Scripture is silent about Elijah's experience of solitude. We assume it was a simple life. Each morning and evening he watched the horizon for the familiar silhouettes of ravens airlifting his next meal. Perhaps his experience studying the skyline enabled him later to recognize the significance of a small cloud the size of a man's hand drifting far on the horizon (1 Kings 18:44-45). Having spent time each day watching for God's ordinary provision prepared Elijah to recognize the onset of God's mighty miracles. Lessons learned in the wilderness find surprising application in our future service.

We might also wonder why God chose to provide food for Elijah twice per day rather than once, as He did with manna for the children of Israel. The Israelites collected sufficient manna each morning to last the remainder of the day. But for Elijah, the morning provision was insufficient for his evening meal. For that, a second visitation was required. Why two provisions per day instead of one? Scripture doesn't tell us, but we can speculate. The unbelieving Israelites were merely being *sustained* in the wilderness in contrast to Elijah who was being *prepared.* The Israelites existed in the wilderness. Elijah was becoming stronger. Twice per day Elijah experienced God's clock-like provision. Never early. Never late. God was preparing Elijah for Mount Carmel where he would have to be absolutely confident that God's provision would arrive precisely on time.

In the wilderness, Elijah also learned that a relationship with God was all he needed. He did not require the companionship of a spouse in order to find happiness. He did not need an attentive staff to feel important. He did not require a large congregation to maintain a healthy self-esteem. He did not even need a close friend with whom to share his burdens. He had God and that was enough. Jesus said that apart from Him, we could do nothing (John 15:5). Yet we often feel as if we need God plus other people in order for us to be happy or successful. The truth is that everything we need to be joyful and content can be found in our relationship with God. Of course, God delights in giving us good gifts, such as a spouse or friends or trusted colleagues, but we should never confuse the gift with the Giver. Gifts can be lost. But when we abide closely with the Giver, we will never be in want. Theologically we know this truth. Nevertheless, we often grow discouraged when people leave or forsake us. We understand God's all-sufficiency intellectually, but often such truths are lost to our heart.

CONCLUSION

God was preparing His servant for one of the most dramatic ministry events in history. For that, Elijah had to be stripped of every edifice and distraction so he could be constructed into a mighty servant of God. We can spend too much time enhancing our life rather than surrendering ourselves. What is left when God strips us bare of every prop and trapping? Are we, as the apostle Paul, content whether we have much or little? (Phil. 4:11). Can we honestly say that if all we have is Christ, we have more than enough? Do we question God's love for us when He allows us to suffer loss? Elijah would discover the answer to these questions while he dwelt in the wilderness.

QUESTIONS TO CONSIDER

1. Are you currently in a wilderness? If so, why might God have assigned you to one? How are you handling it? What have you learned?

2. Has your career seemingly taken a step backwards? How might God be preparing you for something that is to come?

3. How have you handled the "so's" in your life? After you know God's will, what is your typical response? How long does it take for you to obey?

4. At times, have you questioned God's handling of your life? Have you ever been angry with God? If so, why? Have you ever felt that God acted unfairly?

5. Is God enough for you? Do you rely on others for your joy and contentment? Can you be entirely satisfied when you abide in Christ?

CHAPTER THREE

Faithful in Humble Circumstances

"After a while, the wadi dried up because there had been no rain in the land. Then the word of the Lord came to him: 'Get up, go to Zarephath that belongs to Sidon, and stay there. Look, I have commanded a woman who is a widow to provide for you there.' So Elijah got up and went to Zarephath." (1 Kings 17:7-10).

1. WORSENING CIRCUMSTANCES

Assuming the worst is behind you is generally unwise. Many battles have been lost because victory was presumed prematurely. Elijah obediently delivered a difficult sermon. He then remained faithful while abiding in a wilderness. The prophet might have supposed that, having successfully handled his difficult assignments and postings, God would now grant him a task more to his liking. He may have assumed the worst was now behind him and life would return to a more normal, comfortable pattern. Such was not the case.

Scripture does not indicate how many days Elijah dwelt in the wilderness. Perhaps if Scripture revealed that number, we would develop a formula for wilderness dwelling. People who wished to prepare for God's service might spend the same number of days in a self-imposed wilderness so they, too, could have a ministry like Elijah's. But the truth is that the wilderness experience differs for each person. Jesus spent forty days in His wilderness. Others may reside there for years. God will take whatever time is required to prepare His servants for their next assignment. Rushing the process is futile. Don't compare your wilderness sojourn with that of others. Yours will be unique.

The wadi Elijah depended on for water had been dwindling. Day after day as the prophet drank from it, he noticed the creek diminishing to a trickle. One day the flow of water stopped entirely. Living in a wilderness is one thing. Surviving in a wilderness without water is quite another. Elijah's situation had become untenable.

At that moment God spoke to His servant and told him what to do next. *"Then the word of the Lord came to him . . ."* (1 Kings 17:8). Of course, God knew all along that He would eventually send Elijah to Zarephath. God could have informed His servant about his upcoming relocation at any time during his wilderness hiatus. Surely Elijah had wondered about his next assignment. He had to work harder each day to obtain even a modest drink of water from the rapidly disappearing wadi. Yet God remained silent. Elijah was left to make do, one more day, with what God had previously told him.

God's word is a lamp that sheds light on our path (Psalm 119:105). It is delightful each time God dispenses fresh enlightenment on our circumstances. But sometimes we must cling day after day to a previous word He spoke to us. Though we might crave clarification of our circumstances, God may be content to let us continue trusting in the light that, while growing dimmer, still sheds sufficient illumination on our path for us to take the next step. As long as God's previous word keeps us in the center of His will, God may not feel the need to speak a new word of instruction. One of the great tests of God's servants is to see how long they faithfully remain in the last place they heard God tell them to go.

One day the creek dried up. Only then did God give Elijah his next instructions. Why did God wait until the last possible moment to provide guidance to His thirsty prophet? Perhaps because God knew Elijah did not need to know where he was going until it was time to depart. It is human nature to want to know God's will far in advance. We tend to speculate and worry about our future when details are left unclear. Why would God leave His most reliable servant in the dark about his future for so long? Perhaps because doing so left Elijah in a position of total trust in God. Elijah could die in a wilderness without water. Trusting God had become a matter of life or death. This would not be the last time Elijah would find himself in such a position.

2.HUMILIATING OBEDIENCE

"Then the word of the Lord came to him: 'Get up, go to Zaraphath that belongs to Sidon, and stay there. Look, I have commanded a woman who is a widow to provide for you there.' So Elijah got up and went to Zarephath" (1 Kings 17:8-10).

Thus far, each time Elijah faithfully obeyed his Lord, his circumstances grew worse. This pattern will continue into the next stage of Elijah's ministry. First he obediently undertook a difficult assignment and was forced to flee into a wilderness as a result. Then he faithfully trusted God in the wilderness and his water dried up. Now Elijah is told to travel to a Gentile land where Baal worship is the official religion and place his life in the hands of an impoverished widow. Not only would this task be difficult; it would be humiliating.

Widows constituted some of the poorest, most helpless people in society. They could not typically earn a respectable living. Begging or prostitution was generally their only source of livelihood. For a Jewish man, asking for charity from a penniless, widow would have been disgraceful. Yet what God asked was even worse. The widow was a Gentile and a Baal worshipper. Devout Jewish men would never defile themselves by entering the home of a Gentile, and they certainly would never eat food prepared by one.

Zarephath was located near the major city of Sidon, the epicenter of Baal worship and the hometown of Jezebel. We might imagine that, had we been God, we would have provided for our most effective prophet differently. Perhaps we would have guided him to the home of a wealthy God-fearer in the resort town of Jericho, or perhaps to the summer home of a wealthy Israelite by the Sea of Galilee. With all the resources at God's disposal, He surely could have found more comfortable accommodations than the home of a destitute widow. God's methodology continues to surprise us.

Napoleon once claimed that soldiers march on their stomachs. When troops are hungry or thirsty, they are unable to fight. When food supplies are depleted, wise generals retreat until their supply lines are re-established. They do not advance. Once again God is leading His servant to do something that contravenes common logic. Elijah is so impoverished he cannot provide a cup of water for himself. Yet God commands him to advance into the heart of enemy territory! At Elijah's seemingly weakest point, God challenges him to make his most daring move.

3.PERSEVERING OBEDIENCE

"When he arrived at the city gate, there was a widow woman gathering wood. Elijah called to her and said, 'Please bring me a little water in a cup and let me drink.' As she went to get it, he called to her and said, 'Please bring me a piece of bread in your hand.' But she said, 'As the Lord your God lives, I don't have anything baked—only a handful of flour in a jar and a bit of oil in the jug. Just now, I am gathering a couple of sticks in order to go prepare it for myself and my son so we can eat it and die.' Then Elijah said to her, 'Don't be afraid; go and do as you have said. Only make me a small loaf from it and bring it out to me. Afterwards, you may make some for yourself and your son, for this is what the Lord God of Israel says: "The flour jar will not become empty and the oil jug will not run dry until the day the Lord sends rain on the surface of the land."' So she proceeded to do according to the word of Elijah. She and he and her household ate for many days. The jar did not become empty, and the oil jug did not run dry, according to the word of the Lord He had spoken through Elijah" (1 Kings 17:10-16).

When Elijah arrived at the city gate, he may have searched the crowd looking for a widow who had the means to care for an out-of-town guest. When he came upon a widow, he asked for some water. His request was not small. Sidon was experiencing drought. Water was scarce. He was a stranger, from a foreign country. The widow had no obligation to care for him. Yet she immediately agreed to fetch him water. So Elijah made a further, more extravagant request. Would she bring him a small loaf of bread as well? Now he had found her limit. She replied that she was preparing to make one final meal with her remaining food and then starve to death with her son. What must Elijah have thought? He might have assumed that he had apparently stumbled across the wrong widow! God said He would provide for Elijah through a widow. Yet the woman standing before him was impoverished and unable to feed her only son. Clearly this widow must not be the one God intended!

We can sympathize with Elijah. After years of faithful service, he had been reduced to depending on other's charity. Requesting help from a woman was humiliating enough, but a widow? Now it appeared he was to rely on a widow facing imminent starvation. What man would ask someone so pitiful for her remaining food? Elijah might have thought going hungry would be better than taking the last morsel of food from the mouth of a widow and her son. We wonder how we would have responded had we been in Elijah's place. It seems ignoble and ungentlemanly to take from someone so impoverished. Surely God would not ask a person this needy to make such an enormous sacrifice.

Why does God often advance His work through the sacrificial offerings of the humble rather than massive gifts from the wealthy? From our human perspective, asking a widow to give what she could not afford seems unjust, even heartless. And, from a human perspective, it is. But, as we shall see, what at this time appears to be an unfair request of a poor woman will ultimately prove to be the greatest investment of her life.

Elijah asks the woman to bake him a small loaf before she prepares her son's last meal. Why a small loaf? If Elijah is trusting in a miracle for his provision, why not ask for a large loaf? Perhaps because God always grants us what we need, but not always what we want! And further, why does God make use of a widow at all? Since God planned to miraculously provide flour and oil, why did He send it to the widow's pantry? Could God not have continued to convoy His provision through the means of ravens or other creatures? God would later provide a meal for Elijah at the hand of an angel (1 Kings 19:5-8). Could God not have dispatched a heavenly messenger to sustain His hungry prophet? He certainly could. However, God often chooses to provide for His servants through the instrumentality of other people. By working through the widow, God swept her into the middle of His activity, and ultimately saved her and her son. Just as with Jesus and the woman at the well, what first appeared to be God asking for a sacrifice was actually God granting a priceless gift (John 4:7; 14).

As we have seen, the two-letter word "so" weaves the fabric of our life together. Each time God speaks to Elijah, we are told, *"So Elijah arose and went . . ."* Here the widow is asked to take the greatest step of faith in her life. A complete stranger, a foreigner from another country, a person of an entirely different, hostile religion, has just asked her for the last remaining food she planned to feed to her only child. What would she do? Scripture tells us, *"So she proceeded to do according to the word of Elijah"* (1 Kings 17:15). Though she is a poor, humble, Gentile widow, she gives to God's servant what she cannot afford, and thus performs one of the greatest acts of faith recorded in Scripture. She did not know Elijah. She had no idea what her response would cost her son. However, something in her spirit convinced her to trust in Elijah's God. So confident was Elijah in his God, that he convinced this destitute woman to heed God's word too, even though it appeared that such obedience could cost her son's life. Paradoxically, it was by losing her life that she would save it.

Scripture does not indicate how much time Elijah spent in the wilderness or how long he dwelt in the widow's home. The apostle James declares that the drought Elijah announced lasted a total of three years and six months (James 5:17). Perhaps Elijah spent one year in the wilderness. If so, he may have lived with the widow and her son for over two years. We can only speculate. But certainly the prophet spent a significant period of time in that humble home.

Since Jezebel was seeking to arrest and execute God's prophets, we can assume that Zarephath, so close to her hometown, would have been a dangerous place for Elijah to reside. He likely did not spend his time in local cafes and coffee shops! Being surrounded by devout Baal worshippers, Elijah probably remained inside the widow's home. Being seen might have caused scandal on several different levels. As a result, his only companions were the widow and her son.

We must ask again, if we were God, would we have treated our premier prophet in this manner? Elijah was the greatest preacher of his day, yet he was consigned for upwards of three years to a congregation of two people. Why waste a good preacher on such a small congregation? Surely God might have found a better use of His prince of preachers. Yet week after week, month after month, year after year, Elijah's only job was to remain in a modest home and express thanks for his daily meals! To us, this assignment appears to be a waste of God's foremost prophet. But in truth, Elijah was exactly where God intended for him to be.

God's primary concern for His servants is never what they are *doing*, but who they are *becoming*. God can use us in an instant. But changing us generally takes time. Some things cannot be rushed. God had not forgotten Elijah. But for now, Elijah was to wait. For some people, waiting is the most difficult assignment of all. They would rather be commissioned to ascend a mountain, evangelize a pagan nation, or preach to a vast throng than to wait. For them, waiting is excruciating! Some people believe that doing something is always superior to doing nothing. But they are mistaken. Waiting on the Lord is not identical to idleness. Elijah was not merely refraining from activity. He was trusting in the Lord. He was experiencing God's daily provision. He was learning that God loved ordinary people. He was discovering that his effectiveness as a servant was not measured by the size of his congregation but by the depth of his walk with God.

Scripture never indicates that Elijah complained during this period of his life. Perhaps he appreciated having fellowship with humans rather than ravens. He undoubtedly grew fond of the widow and her son. After this time we never hear of Elijah having an ordinary life in a cottage again. What appears to us here to be a hardship might have in fact been a divinely orchestrated oasis in the midst of a frenetic life. Elijah may well have looked back on this time with great fondness as one of the most tranquil and restorative periods of his life. Elijah was learning to trust God in every circumstance. For soon enough, his life would change once again.

CONCLUSION

God is entirely consistent with His character and values. Yet He often acts in ways that are foreign to our thinking. We become confused, not because God acts inconsistently, but because we fail to think the way God does. Elijah might have assumed that when he was residing in a foreign country in the cottage of an impoverished, idol-worshipping widow, he was far removed from God's calling on his life. But in fact, he was in the center of God's will. God is not averse to making us wait. God does some of His greatest work while we are in that humble posture. He takes time to fashion us into the exact instrument He desires. While this process can seem too long in our estimation, God knows that a perfectly designed instrument in the hands of a master craftsman can accomplish enormous feats in a brief time. Our responsibility is to trust our life fully into God's hands until He decides we are ready for the work He has prepared us for. A fully prepared servant in the hands of almighty God is an awesome thing!

QUESTIONS TO CONSIDER

1. Has God currently placed you in a position of need? Why might He have done so? What are you learning?

2. What humbling circumstance has God introduced into your life? Is it having an effect?

3. If you are currently in difficult circumstances, can you see good that is resulting from it? Can you see God's loving hand even in the midst of your hardship?

4. Are you thoroughly content with the assignment God has given you? Are you restless for more? Do you find joy in being faithful to your call, regardless of what your assignment might be?

5. Have you been cherishing the people God has currently put in your life and ministry, or are you discontent until you have more?

CHAPTER FOUR

.

Trusting God for a Miracle

"After this, the son of the woman who owned the house became ill. His illness became very severe until no breath remained in him. She said to Elijah, 'Man of God, what do we have in common? Have you come to remind me of my guilt and to kill my son?'" (1 Kings 17:17-18)

1.REACHING YOUR LIMIT

Few places in Scripture are more laden with anguish than this passage. Throughout this chapter we have journeyed with the prophet as God took him through a series of increasingly difficult challenges. Elijah preached a sermon that seemed likely to land him before an executioner. He endured a harsh, lonely wilderness. Then he trusted God for a miracle in a widow's kitchen. These years were character shaping and faith building. Nevertheless, all his previous difficulties pale in comparison to what the prophet faced next.

A serious illness consumed the widow's son. We are not told how suddenly the illness struck. The boy might have declined in health over several days. Perhaps the widow pleaded with the prophet to pray for her only child to be spared. We can have little doubt that Elijah prayed fervently for his little friend as the boy's health deteriorated. Or perhaps the illness struck suddenly and severely, shocking everyone with its abrupt brutality. Her son's illness was the most devastating crisis that could possibly befall the widow.

We have now reached the climax of this chapter. The widow trusted God's prophet. She took an enormous step of faith by welcoming him into her home. She may have concluded that, by caring for the Lord's servant, the God of Israel would bless her home. She was not yet a believer, but she must have been searching. Now she faced unimaginable tragedy.

Each time Elijah obeyed God, his life became more difficult. After living in poverty with the widow for nearly three years, we might assume God would grant a reprieve to his foremost servant and introduce a greater degree of comfort and ease into his life. Instead, Elijah faced his greatest crisis to date.

Imagine the anguish he felt as the widow, Elijah's only friend, pointed an accusing finger in his face and angrily accused him. After sheltering the hungry prophet and sharing her meager food, the God of Israel rewarded her by allowing her son to die? Was Elijah callously mocking her pagan faith and condemning her unbelief?

We can only imagine the thoughts racing through Elijah's mind. For three years the greatest man of God on the planet had ministered to a congregation of two, yet he had failed thus far to gain a solitary convert. We can be sure that Elijah regularly reminded the woman that Baal was a false, powerless god, and that the God of Israel was the true God. He may have urged her to place her trust in the true God so she could experience His loving-kindness and mercy. We can imagine Elijah assuring her that God loved her and had a wonderful plan for her life.

God certainly could have worked in conjunction with Elijah to convince the woman to believe in Him. Had God used a predictable approach, He might have granted the boy unusual strength and vigor. We would not be surprised had the boy been the most outstanding player on his Little League team or if, like Daniel in a later era, he was far healthier than his peers (Dan. 1:17-20). We might imagine other mothers asking the widow her secret for raising such a robust son. By tangibly blessing the boy, God would have provided compelling evidence to the widow's Baal worshipping neighbors that He was indeed the true God. At least, if we had been God, that is how we might have orchestrated events. Instead, after Elijah grew to know and love his host family, he suddenly lost his little companion to a lethal disease.

This crisis could have been Elijah's breaking point. He had faithfully and courageously weathered earlier storms, but this trial was more severe than any he had previously faced. After three years of struggle, he may have assumed the storms would abate. He would not have anticipated that God would strip him of what little he had left until nothing remained but God.

Should we dare to question God's management of his foremost prophet, we might ask why God did not handle Elijah more gently. After all, Elijah was one of the few people who had not compromised or abandoned his faith. He had diligently obeyed everything God told him to do. Why would God not bless his life and show him favor, rather than allow him to experience ever increasing suffering and loss? Such treatment challenges everything we believe to be right, fair, and good.

Yet, in this moment, we witness the Master skillfully managing His servant. For God understands each person's limit. He made us. He knows our capacity both for suffering and faith. He does not intend to cruelly crush or demoralize us. Yet He also recognizes that, unless He takes us to the end of ourselves, we will never experience the full measure of His grace and power.

Why almighty God allows some of his most effective and faithful servants to suffer grievously is a mystery. Why does He allow a beloved pastor to develop cancer in the prime of his life? Why does God allow faithful missionaries to endure persecution and suffering when they courageously share Christ? Why are godly businesspeople cheated and unfairly dismissed when they behave with integrity and honesty? Moreover, why do virulent atheists and hedonists live long, healthy lives? Why does God allow greedy, unscrupulous businesspeople to enjoy the perks and pay of management positions throughout their tarnished careers? From our limited perspective as creatures of dust, God seems to permit the righteous to suffer too much and the wicked too little.

In truth, we cannot understand all God is doing in the lives of His servants as He leads them through difficult seasons. We do not see how God is burning away dross in their character. We are not privy to the secret sins the Holy Spirit is systematically tracking down and eradicating. We cannot observe the strongholds in even the greatest saints' lives that are being demolished as God allows His servants to endure suffering and unjust treatment. We ought never to assume that God allows suffering that is pointless or ineffectual for His divine purposes. No suffering is wasted. No pain is meaningless. Octavius Winslow observed:

But the true child of the covenant, the Lord tries; the living, fruitful branch, the Husbandman prunes. There is that in every believer, yea, the most eminent child of God,--eminent for his holy and close walk,--that needeth pruning. We cannot always see the *necessity* of the discipline; we wonder, often, why such a believer is so constantly, and, in a sense, so severely dealt with. We look at his godly conversation in all things; we mark his holy deportment, his consistent walk, his lowly spirit, his spiritual gifts and graces, his devotedness and zeal in the cause of the Lord, and we exclaim, "Lord, make me like him, as he is like Thee!" And when we see the cedar in Lebanon bend before the sweeping tempest—when we mark how the man of God becomes the subject of the most overwhelming afflictions, how wave follows wave, and messenger after messenger comes with tidings of evil still more bitter than the last,--when we see this mercy blasted, that comfort removed,--here a check, and there a disappointment, and he whom we gazed upon as one in whom the Lord had deposited great grace, and favored with peculiar nearness and conformity to himself, thus deeply afflicted,--we marvel that the dear Husbandman should prune him as he does. But what says the Husbandman?— "I, the Lord, search the heart." Here is the secret revealed; the *hidden evil* of that holy man of God we could not discover. The powerful corruptions that dwelt in his heart,--and, it may be, judging correctly too, for by their fruits we are to know the true and the false professors,--the Lord was probing and searching the heart, and for the subjugation of the evil that he discovered there, was thus disciplining, and pruning, and purging his beloved child.[1]

We must be cautious in judging God's treatment of His servants. God knows that great service requires extensive preparation. To remove all dross of sin requires purifying fires to be stoked to an intense heat. Saintly service most often flows from great affliction. God planned to use Elijah to bring revival to a sinful, corrupt nation. Elijah would challenge the darkest evil of his nation's history. God does not give such assignments to lukewarm, sin-filled servants. God was willing to go to great lengths to prepare His servant for the epic assignment apportioned to him.

Sadly, many servants give way under pressure. They break right at the point when God's refining fires are about to cool. Had they endured a little longer and continued to trust their Master when their circumstances appeared cruel and unfair, they would have successfully reached the end of the pruning process. But they lost heart and, as a result, never completed the assignment for which God was preparing them. Only heaven knows how many great men and women of God the Church has lost because they could not endure the refining fires God passed them through.

At this point, Elijah was most vulnerable. He had lived in dire poverty. He had been a maligned fugitive. He lost one of his dearest companions. Now his closest friend was accusing him of base cruelty. Yet it is often when we are at our weakest that we are closest to seeing the greatest miracle. Elijah experienced the greatest height in his walk with God on the heels of his lowest ebb.

2.CRYING OUT TO GOD

"But Elijah said to her, 'Give me your son.' So he took him from her arms, brought him up to the upper room where he was staying, and laid him on his own bed. Then he cried out to the Lord and said, 'My Lord God, have you also brought tragedy on the widow I am staying with by killing her son?' Then he stretched himself out over the boy three times. He cried out to the Lord and said, 'My Lord God, please let this boy's life return to him!' So the Lord listened to Elijah's voice, and the boy's life returned to him, and he lived.'" (1 Kings 17:19-22)

The widow held the corpse of her only child while angrily accusing Elijah of being a cruel fraud. What Elijah did next would determine if he had learned the lessons God had been teaching him throughout the last three years. *"Give me your son"* he commanded. Leaving the dead child in his mother's arms and merely announcing he would pray for her might have been easier for the beleaguered prophet. Instead, Elijah took ownership of what happened next. He bore the weight of the suffering himself as he took the boy to his room.

Elijah didn't understand God's purpose for the boy's death. He asked, *"My Lord God, have you also brought tragedy on the widow I am staying with by killing her son?"* God's ways seemed incomprehensible to Elijah. Why would God not help Elijah show the widow God's love and concern for her? God did not appear to be supporting His minister as Elijah faithfully preached to his little congregation. Elijah's only recourse was to pray. He stretched himself over the child three times and cried out to the Lord. We can only imagine the urgency with which Elijah prayed: *"My Lord God, please let this boy's life return to him!"*

This climactic moment in Elijah's journey is laden with meaning. First, we see that he cried out to the Lord. There is a profound difference between saying prayers and crying out to God. God's people are accustomed to saying prayers. We utter them at the commencement and close of worship services. We offer a pithy prayer before we collect the weekly church offering. We hurriedly mutter a prayer before we consume our food. Some still offer a closing prayer before climbing into bed. Throughout the normal course of a day, the average Christian might say half a dozen prayers. Yet, for the most part, nothing of divine significance occurs as a consequence. Christians typically do not expect anything to happen when they pray. As a result, nothing does.

Powerless, fruitless prayer would be utterly inadequate for Elijah. A sanctimonious cliché would have been completely inappropriate. The only thing preventing the tragic death of this beloved child was Elijah's prayer life. There were no medics to summon. There were no elders, deacons, or intercessors to call upon. Elijah's intercession was the last defense standing between his friend and the most devastating crisis of her life. Elijah's final resort was to plead for a miracle. So he cried out to God. Though we have watched Elijah face difficult assignments, a bleak wilderness, and impoverishment, not until now do we find him in a position where he felt obliged to cry out to the Lord. In the past he prayed for a small loaf of bread to eat. Now he was pleading for a dead child to live. Elijah's praying was elevated to a level it had never attained before.

A prayer can be respectable, liturgical, and even poetic. But a cry reflects desperation. We cry when there is nothing left to do. We cry when we know that unless a response is immediately forthcoming, tragedy will ensue. Perhaps that reality is why revival eludes us. Could it be that many of God's servants are saying prayers for revival, but too few are desperately crying out for it?

Second, Elijah stretched himself over the child three times. Why three times? Why not once? The most obvious explanation is that nothing happened after he stretched over the body once. So he did it a second time. Then a third. Clearly, Elijah prayed over the boy three times because that is how many times it took! Had Elijah been required to pray over the boy 49 times, we have no doubt he would have done so. Elijah was not prepared to cease interceding until life returned. How tragic it would have been if, after stretching out over the boy two times, the prophet had given up. Could God have healed the boy after Elijah stretched out over him in prayer once? Certainly. But in God's sovereign will, He chose to withhold his intervention until Elijah prayed three times. We do not understand God's ways. Had we been God, we might have eagerly responded to Elijah's prayer the moment he began, just as He did with Daniel (Dan. 9:23). But God chose to wait until the third time. What if God were to treat us in a similar manner? Would God find us faithfully praying until the answer came?

Scripture notes: *"So the Lord listened to Elijah's voice."* Had God not heard Elijah the first time he prayed? The truth is that God is not obligated to answer us simply because we have uttered words of prayer. God knows everything we do, so He is fully aware of when and what we pray. But we must meet certain requirements before He will respond to our prayers. If there is sin in our heart, He will not answer (Prov. 15:8; Is. 1:15). A broken or strained relationship hinders our prayers (1 Pet. 3:7). We must never assume that because we are praying, God is listening. If our heart is not pure, we must not assume we can burst into God's holy presence and command His attention for our desperate need. God answers prayers on His terms, not ours.

What does God require of people who are praying for a miracle? How large must their faith be? How pure their heart? How urgent their intercession? Elijah had never prayed for the dead to live before. His prayer was entering a realm in which he had never trod. Yet Elijah was not the same man he was at the outset of this story.

He had endured and learned much since God began working in his life.

3. FULLY PREPARED

"Then Elijah took the boy, brought him down from the upper room into the house, and gave him to his mother. Elijah said, 'Look, your son is alive.' Then the woman said to Elijah, 'Now I know you are a man of God and the Lord's word in your mouth is the truth.'" (1 Kings 17:23-24)

Imagine the grin on Elijah's face as he brought the revived boy to his mother. What a celebration must have ensued! This moment may well have been the most joyous in the prophet's life thus far. What had happened?

For one, the widow's faith had finally grown to the point that she placed her faith in Elijah's God. She stated: *"Now I know you are a man of God."* This statement seems peculiar. She had hosted the greatest preacher of that day in her home for upwards of three years, yet she had not believed. She had experienced a daily miracle in her kitchen, yet she remained unconvinced. Perhaps she feared letting go of her lifelong Baal worship. She may have worried about reprisals from neighbors. What finally persuaded the woman? The worst crisis of her life. God allowed her to experience her greatest sorrow in order to gain her most sublime gift. Just as God took Elijah to the limit of himself, God drew the widow to that same place. How far is God willing to let us descend before we finally look up to Him in faith?

God seemed to have expected too much of the impoverished widow. Why ask her to share her food with the Jewish prophet when she did not have enough for herself and her son? And why would God send his premier prophet all the way to Zarephath to find sustenance when there surely must have been Jewish widows who would have willingly ministered to him in Israel? We must conclude that, though God was orchestrating His purposes for national revival in Israel, He also desired that a poor widow and her son, living in the pagan city of Zarephath, come to a saving faith in Him. God chose to conduct His will in such a way that, not only would a nation feel the impact of Elijah's ministry, but so would a Gentile widow in a foreign country. God is perfectly capable of multitasking! He sees the forest, but He never overlooks a solitary tree.

God cares about all people's suffering, including impoverished widows. Had God killed the boy? No. But, God knew that the widow's son would contract a terminal illness. So He dispatched His best prophet. When Elijah asked for a small loaf of bread, she had no idea God would ultimately repay her generosity with the life of her only child. It was no coincidence that when she later faced the most severe crisis in her life, the greatest man of God on the planet occupied her guest room. God is no one's debtor.

Had God been wasting Elijah's life? Had God squandered His greatest preacher with congregations of ravens and a pair of peasants? Clearly not. When we first met Elijah, he was assigned to preach a difficult sermon. From there, God called him to be faithful in a wilderness. Then he demonstrated faith when he was in great need. By the end of this chapter, Elijah is raising the dead. He had come a long way! God enrolled His premier prophet in His school of faith and prayer. Three and a half years later, Elijah had successfully completed the course and was ready for the greatest assignment of his life.

The curtain now drops on this stage of Elijah's life. He had experienced a difficult period, but it eventually ended, as such periods generally do. Where do we find him in the subsequent chapter? On Mount Carmel, facing 850 false prophets in a titanic showdown. On one side stood 850 idol-worshipping prophets, the evil king Ahab, and his henchmen. On the other side stood one lone prophet. The situation might have appeared utterly hopeless had Elijah not just graduated from God's school of faith and prayer.

All day the priests of Baal pleaded with their god to answer with fire, but heaven remained silent. Finally Elijah's turn came. He knew he would meet a gruesome end if his next prayer went unanswered. Yet he was so confident that he instructed people to douse the altar with water three times. Then he prayed. His was not a desperate prayer, even though his life hung in the balance. He did not pray verbosely, eloquently, or loudly.

He simply spoke to the God he had served throughout the last three-and-a-half years. And fire fell! How could Elijah be so certain fire would fall? He had just experienced three-and-a-half years of God's daily, clock-like provision. God had not failed him once, even when he needed a miracle. Elijah knew God wouldn't fail him this time either.

CONCLUSION

Many Christians have wished for a ministry as powerful as Elijah's. Oh how ministers have longed for heavenly fire to fall on their church! There is no shortage of volunteers prepared to be the Elijah for their generation. Yet as we have seen, people do not become Elijahs overnight. God took three-and-a-half years to prepare His servant for his next assignment. The training was rigorous. The disappointments seemed never-ending. Yet, when God was finished, He had a mighty prophet at His disposal. How long would you be willing to remain in God's hand until He was satisfied that you, too, were prepared to undertake His mighty work?

QUESTIONS TO CONSIDER

1. Are you currently facing a need that requires a miracle? How are you handling it?

2. Has your faith in God grown over the last three years? If so, what is the evidence?

3. Has your prayer life grown over the last three years? If so, in what way? If not, why not?

4. Have you persevered in prayer until God's answer came?

5. Have you been saying prayers or crying out to God? What does that reflect about your walk with God and your understanding of the issues you face?

6. Are you prepared to remain in God's school of faith and prayer until you are fully prepared for the next assignment God has for you?

---

[1]Octavius Winslow, *Personal Declension and Revival of Religion in the Soul* (Eugene, Oregon: Wipf and Stock Publishers, n.d.). First published in 1841. 155-156.

SECTION TWO

Elijah: Restored at Mount Sinai

INTRODUCTION

The vast majority of human existence consists of ordinary living. Occasionally, however, people are granted the opportunity to achieve something extraordinary. These are life's high water moments. It might be the year they lead their company in sales, or when they are promoted to management. Perhaps it is a child's birth or wedding. It could be achieving notable success in a sport, field of expertise, or area of self-mastery. People's greatest achievements often define them for the remainder of their lives.

People peak at different points. Some achieve major accomplishments in their youth. They might be a sports phenomenon in college or achieve a remarkable breakthrough early in their careers. With their reputation established, they spend the remainder of their lives basking in the fading glory of years gone by. Others, like Noah, Abraham, and Moses, do not achieve their life's greatest accomplishment until they are senior citizens.

As youth, we assume our future holds many adventures and successes. But as we grow older, we begin to wonder if the remainder of our life will ultimately be disappointing or anti-climactic. According to legend, Alexander the Great wept when he reached the limits of the known world because nothing remained for him to conquer. As a young man, Julius Caesar grieved when he realized that, though he had as yet accomplished nothing of significance, by his age, Alexander the Great had already conquered the known world.

Some people are unconcerned with their life's accomplishments. They merely want to experience happiness, earn a living, or endure another day. But most people eventually wonder, "Have I already experienced God's best for my life? Is there anything else? Are my best days behind me? Does God have anything of significance left for me to do?"

Such was the case with Elijah. He had reached a critical juncture. His life had not been easy, but he had experienced dramatic success. Now, however, his future looked uncertain. Preparing for a great undertaking is one thing. Continuing to find meaning in life *after* a significant accomplishment is another. Elijah spent three-and-a-half years preparing for Mount Carmel. When that day came, it exceeded everyone's expectations. But it was now over. Rising out of bed each morning can be challenging when you sense your best days are behind you.

Elijah would learn that, when God is the author of our life, there is always another exciting chapter still to come. While our future experiences may differ from those in our past, they continue to be significant because it is God who initiates them.

Mountains defined Elijah's life. He found fame on Mount Carmel. He experienced restoration atop Mount Sinai. We last see him in Scripture on the Mount of Transfiguration, communing with Moses and the Messiah. Oh that our life was a series of mountain peaks! How glorious that would be! But alas, spaced between those summits are desolate valleys and barren wildernesses. The higher we climb on the mountain, the lower into the valley we must inevitably descend.

Surprisingly, some of history's noblest saints have suffered during their valley sojourns. They struggled not because God was inactive, but because God had previously acted so powerfully in their life. Once we experience God's awesome power working through us on the mountaintop, returning to ordinary living in the valley can be tedious. We often stereotype saints as those who crested far above the masses during momentous occasions. But what often separates spiritual giants from ordinary Christians is how they handle life's mundane moments. For some, it is far easier to charge into a fierce battle in the name of the Lord than to suffer constant criticism in a barren wilderness.

The key is not our circumstances, but our God. A vibrant walk with God can sustain us in every situation. Elijah learned this lesson once. He would have to learn it again.

CHAPTER FIVE

A Vulnerable Moment

"Ahab told Jezebel everything that Elijah had done and how he had killed all the prophets with the sword." (1 Kings 19:1)

1.VICTORY!

Rarely had the powers of darkness been so thoroughly lured out of their strongholds and summarily defeated. God won a singular victory through Elijah. Similar feats occasionally occurred under the rule of godly monarchs such as Jehoshaphat, Hezekiah, and Josiah, but no one could have imagined such a remarkable triumph of righteousness during the exceedingly wicked reign of king Ahab.

Elijah convinced Ahab to summon all of the prophets of Baal and Asherah to Mount Carmel for a climactic showdown (1 Kings 18:19-20). There, the prophet threw down the gauntlet to his countrymen, saying: *"How long will you hesitate between two opinions? If Yahweh is God, follow Him. But if Baal, follow him"* (1 Kings 18:21). Then Elijah engaged in an epic battle between good and evil.

Satan, the father of lies, deceives people into trusting him and rejecting God (John 8:44). Yet he is typically wary of being drawn into a headlong test of strength with almighty God, for his lies are no match for God's truth. Rather than engage in a frontal assault on righteousness, evil generally uses more devious means. It clings to government power. It uses force rather than truth, to coerce people into submission. Throughout history, false religions have bullied, threatened, and seduced people to submit to its rule. Any religion or philosophy that relies on force to obtain followers proves that heaven and truth are not its allies.

In an unprecedented encounter, Elijah drew the powers of darkness into heaven's light while the nation watched. We admire Elijah's brashness as he taunted the false prophets, suggesting that their god was sleeping or indisposed (1 Kings 18:26-29). Openly antagonizing the minions of darkness who loathed Elijah and longed to exterminate him required enormous courage.

Finally, Elijah's turn came. So confident was he that God would send fire from heaven to consume his sacrifice that he instructed the people to douse the altar with water three times. Elijah ensured there was no other explanation for what happened next except God's glorious intervention.

Then Elijah prayed. How does one pray when asking for an unprecedented miracle? Should you use grandiose language? Should you shout? Should you plead? Elijah simply said: "*Lord God of Abraham, Isaac, and Israel, today let it be known that You are God in Israel and that I am Your servant, and that at Your word I have done all these things. Answer me, Lord! Answer me so that this people will know that You, Yahweh, are God and that You have turned their hearts back*" (1 Kings 18:36-37). Then comes that awesome phrase: "*Then Yahweh's fire fell*" (1 Kings 18:38).

Elijah had the audacity to put his faith on display before a watching world. The result? When the people saw God's answer to Elijah's entreaty, "*they fell facedown and said, 'Yahweh, He is God! Yahweh, He is God!'*" (1 Kings 18:39). One person's unwavering faith convinced an entire nation of God's power, while eradicating the chief proponents of the most prolific false religion. The odds had been 850 to one. However, when God is with the one, one is a majority!

As amazing as Elijah's day had been, God was not yet finished. Once God has us in the condition and position He desires, there is much He can accomplish! Elijah ascended to the summit of Mount Carmel and began to pray. God had just brought judgment on the false prophets of Baal and Asherah. However, God's purging always makes room for blessing. God never removes something without seeking to replace it with something better. Now that the prophets of Baal were gone, God took center stage.

Elijah prayed seven times before the rain began to fall (1 Kings 18:43). In Zarephath, Elijah prayed over a dead child three times before his entreaty was answered (1 Kings 17:21). In summoning heavenly fire, Elijah only had to pray once. Elijah's prayers were so powerful that God used them to raise the dead and end droughts. Nevertheless, God did not always respond after Elijah's initial request. Occasionally even the mighty prophet Elijah had to ask more than once. Elijah's sojourn in Zarephath had taught him that when his initial prayer was not answered, he should pray again, and again. Elijah prayed three times before God restored the boy to life. Elijah learned not to lose heart in prayer, but to persevere. This time he prayed three times and yet no rain was forthcoming. So he prayed a fourth time, and then a fifth and sixth. Undaunted, Elijah prayed seven times before God's answer arrived in a deluge.

In one remarkable day, a nation received incontrovertible proof of God's existence, the chief proponents of a false religion were silenced, and a three-and-a-half-year-old drought came to an end. It was a high water mark for Israel and the climax of Elijah's career.

Oh that every servant of God would strike at least one blow for the kingdom of God! How different the world would be today if Christians boldly challenged the darkness that permeated their community. Elijah faced evil head-on and the result was spectacular. Had the story ended here, Elijah would enter the pages of history as an invincible, miracle-working champion of God. But of course, his story continues, and in the days following he will provide incontrovertible evidence that he is a man with a nature very much like ours (James 5:17).

2. AFTER THE VICTORY

Some people spend so much time focusing on upcoming battles that they are unprepared for the ensuing triumph. We generally spend little time planning for what we will do after we achieve success. Perhaps God would grant us greater accomplishments if only we were more astute at handling them.

Elijah spent more than three years preparing for his divinely appointed tasks atop Mount Carmel. Though spectacular, his mountaintop ministry only lasted one day. The dreary years of drought had brought the apostate king Ahab and his minions to their knees. During that same gloomy season, God simultaneously fashioned His servant Elijah into a powerful instrument.

Many people today are praying for revival. They typically assume that because they yearn for a mighty moving of God's Spirit across their land, they will be prepared when it comes. Yet desiring something does not mean we are prepared for it. After spending years in the wilderness and in the widow's home, Elijah may have been anxious to finally return to "active" duty. He may have longed to preach once more or to engage in strategic ministry. Any divine assignment might have seemed more desirable than merely saying grace over another humble meal in the widow's home. Nevertheless, God refused to rush the process. He took no shortcuts to equipping His prophet. Sure enough, when God finally dispatched Elijah to Mount Carmel, the result exceeded everyone's expectations.

Our expectations often get us into trouble. We envision the fruit of our service. We imagine how people will respond to our efforts. We assume our situation will improve and people will be grateful for what we accomplish. But these assumptions often lead to disappointment. The wise servant of God refrains from jumping to conclusions. Predicting how people will behave is foolhardy, for people are highly unpredictable. They do not always act sensibly. They often fail to conform to logic, despite compelling evidence. Sin can blind the most brilliant people and incite them to act imprudently, even cruelly. We would be disappointed much less often if we made fewer assumptions about God or people.

Once the drought ended and the rains began to descend, God empowered Elijah to run seventeen miles from Mount Carmel to Jezreel (1 Kings 18:46). King Ahab had withdrawn to Jezreel where Jezebel awaited him in their palace (1 Kings 21:1). We are uninformed why God dispatched Elijah to Jezreel, but we can speculate what Elijah might have thought. King Ahab had just witnessed God hurling fire down from heaven as a result of Elijah's prayer. Then Ahab saw a prolonged drought end as a result of the prophet's intercession. Now Elijah had come to the royal city. It would be an opportune moment to negotiate a ceasefire and come to a mutual understanding. Clearly God was on Elijah's side and it was exceedingly unwise to continue waging war against him. Perhaps God, in His grace, was making His prophet available to Ahab should he choose to repent of his sin. If God could forgive the king of Nineveh, or show mercy to the king of Babylon, then He could also forgive Ahab (Jon. 3:5-10; Dan. 4:34-37).

We do not know what Elijah expected, but we assume he anticipated a dramatically different result than what occurred. Rarely had people received such vivid proof of God's might. Now that God had acted, a response was required. There were three primary reactions that affected Elijah and his ministry: the peoples', his enemies', and God's.

The people. Initially, the people's response to Elijah's ministry appeared better than he could have hoped. They witnessed heavenly fire and immediately burst into uproarious praise for the true God. They subsequently followed Elijah's instructions and executed the pagan prophets at the Brook Kishon (1 Kings 18:40). This must have encouraged Elijah, for the people appeared to be turning from their sinful ways and returning to God. Preachers long to witness such an enthusiastic response to their public ministry.

But then the people went silent. The loud, joyous praise and declarations of loyalty to God subsided. The people returned to their homes and routines and abandoned Elijah. We have no record of anyone thanking Elijah for his bold, uncompromising preaching. No invitations to dinner were forthcoming. No one asked Elijah for further instructions. There was a resounding, eerie, deafening silence.

Such has been the unfortunate lot of many of God's spokespeople. After the music subsided and the crowds dispersed, the lone preacher wondered if the worship service made any lasting difference. Even as people shook the minister's hand and exclaimed, "I really enjoyed your sermon today!", the minister mused if the people would remember his message the following morning. The only thing more demoralizing than working with difficult people is ministering to such people and experiencing negligible results. Woe to God's servant whose motivation derives from the appreciative response of congregants, for that path surely leads to disappointment and disillusionment.

Elijah's *enemies*. Elijah was keenly aware of his enemies. He lived in unusually wicked times. But like any faithful minister, he must have hoped that, given enough compelling evidence, his opponents would recognize God's hand upon him and turn from their wicked ways.

Perhaps when his enemies witnessed his zeal for God, they would finally give him the benefit of the doubt and make peace with him. Perhaps after his opponents saw the clear evidence of God's work, they would finally accept Elijah's message. However, if our friends fail to support our efforts on behalf of the Lord, then we certainly ought to be judicious in what we expect from our enemies.

Modern society has witnessed the rise of virulent atheists who loudly proclaim that Christianity has buried its head in the sand of faith and is unwilling to face scientific truth. They make this argument while disregarding the fact that many of the world's greatest scientists have been devout Christians. Ironically, many of these secularists are close-minded to facts that challenge their theories. For many, no amount of evidence will dissuade them from their disbelief in God. They adamantly resolve not to believe. Many of Christianity's opponents are clearly not motivated by a pursuit of truth, but by zeal to vindicate their own values, beliefs, and lifestyles. Such was the case with Ahab and Jezebel.

This showdown on Mount Carmel was to be the definitive test case to prove once and for all whether the God of Israel or Baal was the true deity. Who would not want to witness such a contest? Who was noticeably absent? Jezebel.

Jezebel was the driving force behind Baal worship in Israel. She funded 850 false prophets at her own expense (1 Kings 18:19). We might expect that Jezebel would be most anxious to have her priests vindicated and Elijah's teachings repudiated. But she was absent. We are told, *"Ahab told Jezebel everything that Elijah had done"* (1 Kings 19:1).

Why was Jezebel not present at Carmel to prove the veracity of her beliefs? Because she had no desire to have her beliefs affirmed, adjusted, or attacked. The sad truth is, not even fire falling dramatically from heaven will change a heart that is determined not to believe. Elijah orchestrated one of the greatest proofs of God's existence in human history, and his primary critic chose to stay home. After the spectacular miracles both of fire and rain, God dispatched His top prophet to the neighborhood of Ahab and Jezebel's palace, but they declined to even invite him in for tea. God's servants must accept the harsh reality that there will be those who will relentlessly oppose them, regardless of how spectacular their ministry may be.

God. Thus far, God has always spoken to Elijah when he needed further instruction. Whenever God was silent, Elijah proceeded with the last word he had heard. When no new word of instruction was forthcoming in the wilderness, Elijah held fast, continuing his newfound hobby of bird watching. When a fresh word was not forthcoming in Zarapheth, Elijah continued to abide in the widow's home, faithfully giving thanks for every meal. Eventually God spoke and Elijah had his marching orders once more.

At Mount Carmel, God answered Elijah's prayers with fire and rain from heaven, right on schedule. Then God dispatched His servant seventeen miles to the royal city of Jezreel. It appeared that Elijah was finally on the brink of an enormous breakthrough. Every new word from God seemed more exciting than the last. National revival appeared imminent. God had dispatched him to the city of the king. Surely a royal summons was imminent. But then heaven went silent. The crowds dispersed. The king returned to his queen. Yet no new word from God was forthcoming.

God's silences can be unnerving. They force us to wait, and listen. They synchronize us with heaven's timetable. They reveal the level of our trust in God. But they do something else. The silences of God provide opportunities for contradictory voices to step forward and demand an audience. While God remained silent in Jezreel, another voice captured Elijah's attention. It would be that voice of darkness that would drive him to the brink of ruin.

3. SPIRITUAL RETALIATION

"So Jezebel sent a messenger to Elijah, saying, 'May the gods punish me and do so severely if I don't make your life like the life of one of them by this time tomorrow!'" (1 Kings 19:2).

Be absolutely certain of this: regardless of the magnitude of God's accomplishment, the powers of darkness will inevitably offer a rebuttal. For Elijah, retaliation came quickly and decisively. While Elijah waited in Jezreel for God's next word of instruction, Queen Jezebel sent a devastating missive. She threatened that by the following day Elijah would meet a gruesome death. There would be no discussion or compromise. The opening salvo had been fired and now Jezebel's forces would unleash their own cannonade.

Scripture does not reveal what Elijah expected of Ahab and Jezebel, but clearly he was unprepared for this reaction. It unhinged him. For the first time we witness Elijah behaving in an uncharacteristically fearful and defeated manner. Jezebel's response struck his Achilles heel. Elijah now took matters into his own hands.

The veteran prophet was in Jezreel, near the king's palace. It became clear that, rather than return the nation back to following the Lord, the king and queen would be more zealous than ever to silence anyone who upheld God's truth. Soldiers may already have been dispatched to apprehend the royal family's chief nemesis. In a panic, Elijah fled into the wilderness.

A word from God sent Elijah to a mountaintop. A word from Jezebel sent him fleeing into the desert!

When Elijah based his life on God's word, there was a serenity and peace about his life, even when he faced difficult circumstances. But now his actions are being driven by the voices of people. And not just any people but his worst enemy. When you allow your enemy rather than God to set the agenda for your life, you are in a perilous position!

What caused Elijah to abandon the field of battle? How could a miracle-working prophet such as he be so thoroughly disarmed?

Elijah had been living as a fugitive. Every time a horse and rider appeared on the horizon, he wondered if Ahab's henchmen were coming to seize him. Odd sounds in the night reminded him that ever-present danger was near. Yet throughout his exile, Elijah stoically accepted his lot. Nevertheless, Elijah would not have been human had he not hoped that one day his circumstances would improve. Surely he hoped that his enemies would eventually relent from their animosity toward him or recognize the futility of continuing to wage war against God's anointed. If nothing else, Elijah might have hoped God would allow Jezebel to contract a terminal disease or Ahab to be slain in battle. Elijah must have imagined that if he held on just a little longer, and if his ministry experienced just a little more success, his life would gradually become peaceful and prosperous again.

How many ministers have futilely grasped at hope, like Elijah, that with enough time and faithful ministry, circumstances in their church would change? If only they preached enough sermons on godliness. If only the church scheduled a revival meeting. If only they met with their opponents and shared their heart with them. If only they prayed fervently and enlisted others in the church to intercede. If only the church grew in attendance and saw its offerings increase. Then their opponents would realize the error of their ways and be reconciled.

But, after attendance grew substantially, the budget was met, a second service was added, and a glorious revival meeting conducted, the deacons called a special meeting and insisted that the pastor resign immediately. The result is often just as devastating as it was for Elijah.

Many people in the congregation loved and appreciated their minister, yet the threat of a few was enough to drive him from the church. Many lives have been transformed through the pastor's ministry, yet a handful of hardened, carnal members dominate his thoughts. Though many of the church members love and appreciate the pastor, the minister will often choose to resign from the church rather than engage in battle. The minister justifies his withdrawal because he does not want to drag the congregation into an ugly conflict or have his family endure the inevitable unpleasantness if he remains.

The sad result is that ungodly church members retain control of the church while God's servant withdraws into a wilderness. Elijah was not the last servant of God to be disheartened by an evil person's threat. Many ministers have walked in his shoes.

Elijah's case is particularly enlightening. On the one hand, Jezebel is not a typical cranky congregant. She was responsible for the murder of dozens of people just like Elijah. Hers was no idle threat. On the other hand, Elijah had just prayed down an inferno from heaven. His ministry was characterized by fire! Later, a king will twice dispatch fifty soldiers to capture Elijah, and the prophet will rain fire down on their heads (2 Kings 1:10-12). Surely Elijah could have done the same to Jezebel's assassins. But Elijah has been unnerved.

Moreover, Jezebel will prove that not all threats come to pass. She vowed that Elijah would be dead within twenty-four hours. She claimed she would die if Elijah did not. But this was false. Jezebel spoke two untruths, yet her lies dismantled Elijah. Being undone by an enemy's active opposition is one thing. Being defeated by an opponent's threats and lies is another.

Something about Jezebel and her tone disarmed Elijah. For the first time, Elijah encountered someone as fervent for evil as he was for righteousness. He discovered that evil never grows weary. It never sleeps. It never loses heart. No matter how decisively good overcomes evil, the following day finds evil back at its devilish tricks. Over time, this reality can demoralize even the most stouthearted servant of God.

Elijah had just experienced the greatest spiritual triumph of his life. Yet one word from his enemy propelled him into a headlong retreat. How quickly we can descend from the heights to the depths! How rapidly our victory can morph into defeat! We all have our weaknesses. Certain types of people, at particular times, under specific circumstances, can find us most vulnerable. On a different day, Elijah might have brushed off such a threat from Jezebel with hardly a thought. But not that day. Not after what Elijah had endured. Not after what Elijah had hoped. Elijah is the greatest prophet in the Bible. He has just prayed fire down from heaven before a watching nation. He has just altered weather patterns as a result of his prayers. Yet remarkably, in a moment of weakness, this prophet of fire turned and ran for his life into the desert, resigning from every office as he went.

We do well to heed Elijah's example. Years of faithful service can be dismantled when an attack, temptation, or crisis strikes us at a vulnerable moment. We must diligently guard our heart, for it is a fickle ally. At one moment it is a fierce warrior, driving us to glorious heights. The next instant it grows weak and abandons us, opening the gate to the enemy.

CONCLUSION

Elijah's example teaches us a crucial truth: we cannot minister with yesterday's walk with God. Our relationship with God must remain fresh. It requires daily renewal. Our walk with the almighty will grow stale if unattended. We must not assume that our bold faith of yesterday undergirds our service today. When our walk with God is neglected, it soon weakens. Having witnessed Elijah boldly taunting 850 false prophets on Mount Carmel, we are stunned to see how quickly his faith and courage dissipates. But lest we be too quick to cast stones at the vacillating prophet, such is our nature as well.

QUESTIONS TO CONSIDER

1. Have you experienced disappointment in serving God? If so, what was the cause? Do you tend to set unrealistic expectations?

2. What is your Achilles heel? What generally discourages you?

3. Have you grown weary in well doing (Galatians 6:9)?

4. How well have you handled success? Have you properly prepared for it?

5. In what ways has your experience been like that of Elijah?

6. How difficult has it been for you to keep your faith in God and your love for Him fresh and vibrant each day?

CHAPTER SIX

Withdrawing to God

1.RETURNING TO THE WILDERNESS

"Then Elijah became afraid and immediately ran for his life. When he came to Beersheba that belonged to Judah, he left his servant there, but he went a day's journey into the wilderness" (1 Kings 19:3-4).

Multiple paths lead to the wilderness. One means of entry, as we have seen, is when God leads you to withdraw into the wilderness for a specific purpose. Though God may have used people to orchestrate your sequestration, it is ultimately divinely inspired. There, in quiet solitude, God prepares you for what He knows is coming. In such cases, the wilderness is beneficial as God performs a necessary work.

But there are other entryways into the wilderness. The Israelites in Moses' day became so afraid of the Canaanites that they refused to enter the Promised Land. Their fear cost them forty years in a wilderness (Num. 14:26-45). Moses's anger toward an Egyptian cost him forty years in a wilderness (Ex. 2:11-15). The wilderness was not necessarily God's original plan. Nevertheless, God used it to rehabilitate His servants so He could use them again.

The first time Elijah entered a wilderness, God assigned him to it (1 Kings 17:2). This time, Elijah takes up residence of his own volition because he is afraid. Fear is a primary cause of wilderness dwelling. Although fear is a widespread human malady, God is not its author (2 Tim. 1:7). The only fear God encourages is reverence for Him (Deut. 6:2; Ps. 33:8; 111:10; Luke 12:54). Unfortunately, God's people have generally feared people too much and God too little.

God continually urges people not to be afraid (Josh. 1:9; Judges 6:23; 2 Kings 19:6; Mark 6:50). He knows fear distorts our view of reality and magnifies our problems. It also blurs our vision of God and His might. The larger our fear becomes, the smaller God appears. Elijah had just witnessed almighty God sending fire from heaven. Yet fear now caused him to doubt that God could protect him from one evil woman.

Fear is a confusing human condition. It strikes people differently. Some dread heights, others spiders. Certain types of situations, like speaking in public, terrify some people but invigorate others. The key is to understand what fears we still need to surrender to God. We can be certain of this: our enemies will not relent until they discover our fears and manipulate them against us. Fear prevents ordinary people from becoming great. Fear robs people of God's blessing. Fear is humanity's unrelenting, merciless thief. It bullies people into surrendering hope, losing confidence, and giving up. Even great leaders and saints have fears. Eventually, life uncovers them, just as it did with Elijah.

2. QUITTING

"He sat down under a broom tree and prayed that he might die. He said, 'I have had enough! Lord, take my life, for I am no better than my fathers. Then he lay down and slept under the broom tree" (1 Kings 19:4-5).

Overcome by fear, Elijah fled over one hundred miles into the wilderness. Arriving at Beersheba, he dismissed his servant and kept going. One of the dangers of withdrawing is, once we begin, it is difficult to stop. Beersheba is the southernmost city in Judah. It is where the patriarch Isaac once dwelt. Isaac's son Jacob disgraced himself by cheating his brother and lying to his father in Beersheba. It was where Jacob abandoned God's promises and withdrew from the Promised Land (Gen. 28:10). Now, centuries later, Beersheba was where Elijah abandoned God's call on his life and fled into exile.

By dismissing his servant, Elijah was announcing that he no longer needed assistance, since he was quitting the prophetic ministry. Then he journeyed another day, deeper into the wasteland. Clearly Elijah was not intending a brief hiatus. He was withdrawing as far from his divine calling as he possibly could, with no apparent plans to return. He was also distancing himself from the last remaining human voice. We might assume that at such a dark time, Elijah would appreciate having at least one remaining friend to console him. However, people often prefer to suffer in isolation. Elijah may not have wanted anyone to analyze his actions. He had no desire to answer awkward questions about why he was abandoning God's call. A sure sign we are descending into the morass of self-pity is when we isolate ourselves from those who might question our actions. The attraction of the wilderness is that the only voice we have to listen to is our own. Our actions make perfect sense, as long as no one challenges them.

Quitting makes a more powerful theological statement than does our creed. We may adamantly declare our belief in an omnipotent God, but giving up exposes our conviction that God is not powerful enough to bring victory. We may uphold the doctrine that God is all loving. Yet by quitting His assignment for us, we declare our belief that God cannot be trusted. Quitting announces in no uncertain terms that with God, all things are *not* possible.

Elijah had declared to King Ahab that the God of Israel lived. Yet by quitting his ministry, he was acting as if God was dead. Elijah was also making a declaration about his prophetic calling. He was behaving as if his vocation was his own, not God's. God had not released him from his calling. God had not declared his assignment was complete. God had not acknowledged that Elijah's task was too difficult. Elijah had unilaterally deserted his post without first consulting with his Lord.

Many of God's servants have felt divinely called to a particular assignment. At the outset, they clearly discerned God's leading to their place of service and they enthusiastically embraced His will. Yet, when difficulties arose, opposition attacked, and disappointments mounted, these people abandoned their post. Discouraged, wounded, and assailed, they assumed their position was untenable and they had no choice but to withdraw.

What God's servants must resolve is that if God calls you, only He can dismiss you. Servants do not abandon their assignment when difficulties arise. Only their master can reassign them or permit them to withdraw. People must beware of taking charge of their divine service. Servants do not negotiate terms for their labor. They simply obey. We must not assume that because people attack us, criticize us, or refuse to help us, that we are entitled to quit. All others may retreat in the heat of battle, but God's servants remain at their post.

Elijah was certainly not a fainthearted follower of God. But even he had his limit, and at last he reached it. Nevertheless, though you can quit a job, you cannot cancel your calling.

Elijah was weary. He was tired of ministering to stubborn, wicked, and unreliable people. He was sick of unrelenting evil. He wanted to withdraw and rest. He cried out: *"I have had enough! Lord, take my life, for I am no better than my fathers"* (1 Kings 19:4). Elijah was so discouraged he claimed he wanted to die. We know of course that his claim was untrue. Had he wanted to die, he could have simply remained in Jezreel and Jezebel's henchmen would have happily accommodated him. Elijah was running because he didn't want to die. However, he also didn't want his life to continue as it was.

At times, God changes our circumstances to enable us to better manage our load. On other occasions, rather than change our situation, God changes us. Though our life remains difficult, God grants us the grace and strength to endure it. In those instances, God alters our vision rather than our venue. Though the circumstances remain the same, we are encouraged to carry on now that we see our life from God's vantage point. Elijah's plea for death is a cry to God for help. Such a plea is never ignored in heaven.

Alone in the wilderness under a broom tree, Elijah went to sleep. Sleep certainly provided much needed physical rejuvenation, but it did more than that. It also helped Elijah forget about his problems. When he was sleeping he did not have to consider what to do next or how to respond to his relentless enemies. It was an escape.

While God intends for His servants to receive adequate rest, God is anything but an escapist. He never avoids issues or problems. He refuses to close His eyes and ignore difficult circumstances. Neither does He allow His servants to do so. For a Christian servant, rest is always for preparation, never for flight.

Elijah might have assumed that by traveling deep into the wilderness he was exempt from continued service. He may have concluded that he was too far removed from his calling for God to have any further use for him. But Elijah would learn that God takes His promises extremely seriously. We may give up on Him, but He never gives up on us. We may lose hope, but He cannot. We may forego God's calling on our life, but God will continue to pursue His purposes. We may run from God, but He will find us every time.

When Jacob left Beersheba centuries earlier, he may have assumed he had failed God so miserably that there was no hope for him. But in his weakest, lowest moment, he had a profound encounter with God. In a heavenly vision, Jacob saw God standing atop a heavenly ladder, marshaling angels to and fro as they carried out His bidding (Gen. 28:12). On that fateful night, Jacob learned that, though he might give up on God, God would never give up on him. As he composed himself from that encounter, Jacob declared: *"Surely the Lord is in this place, and I did not know it. . . What an awesome place this is! This is none other than the house of God. This is the gate of heaven."* (Gen. 28:16-17).

Elijah would soon discover, as Jacob had, that when we are at our lowest point, we are often closer to God than we could ever have imagined.

3. PREPARED TO RETURN

"Suddenly, an angel touched him. Then he looked, and there at his head was a loaf of bread baked over hot stones and a jug of water. So he ate and drank and lay down again. Then the angel of the Lord returned a second time and touched him. He said, 'Get up and eat, or the journey will be too much for you.' So he got up, ate, and drank. Then on the strength from that food, he walked 40 days and 40 nights to Horeb, the mountain of God." (1 Kings 19:5-8)

God's suddenness takes our breath away. Scripture regularly uses the word "suddenly" when referring to God's work in people's lives. God's activity appears sudden because it is unexpected. God acts in ways, places, and at times we do not anticipate. When we abide in Christ, we are prepared for God to act. When we are disoriented to Him, His actions surprise us.

Elijah had travelled a great distance. At any point in his journey, the angel could have accosted him. But heaven remained silent. Not until Elijah stopped running did he finally hear from God. God is infinitely astute at knowing the optimum moment to address His servants. When they are fleeing they can be deaf to His voice and immune to His touch. At last Elijah had become still. And, it is in stillness that God delights to engage His servants (Ps. 46:10).

The apostle James exhorts: *"Draw near to God, and He will draw near to you"* (James 4:8). At certain points in our life, we may realize we have drifted in our walk with God and it is time for us to return. But though we may have orchestrated our departure, we need God's help to return. We can leave God on our terms. We can only return on His.

Elijah was awakened by the touch of an angel. What must have gone through the frightened prophet's mind? Before going to sleep he had pleaded with God to let him die. Then he awakened to the smell of fresh baked bread and the gentle touch of an angel. God had not forgotten him! Though Elijah was far from where he should have been, God found him.

God's use of angels is informative. God frequently dispatches heavenly messengers to prepare people for their divine assignment. For example, God sent an angel to Gideon to instruct him to lead the Israelites to overthrow the occupying Midianite army (Judg. 6:11–24). Gideon was so afraid of his enemies he was hiding in a wine press. Even after the angel delivered his message, the timid farmer required numerous assurances before he acted. We wonder why God went to such great lengths to enlist this reluctant deliverer. Why would God not simply send the angel directly to the Midianites? On some occasions, God used angels with devastating effect against Israel's enemies (2 Kings 19:35; 2 Chron. 21:14-17). Yet most of the time when we glimpse at angels in the Bible, they are playing a supportive role. Undoubtedly, angels could serve God more effectively, powerfully, and enthusiastically than people do. We can imagine almighty God calling for volunteers in heaven to undertake a divine assignment. Instantly, legions of angels would eagerly volunteer for the unparalleled privilege of serving their Creator. From a practical standpoint, using angels rather than people would seem to be more efficient. They would not hesitate or argue or debate. They would respond promptly. We do not understand God's reasoning. But one thing is clear. God often chooses to use human instruments on earth, even when they are far more fragile, unreliable, and fearful than heavenly hosts. Elijah's angel might have been a far steadier and reliable messenger at this time, but he was not allowed to deny Elijah the awesome privilege of serving his Lord. Though the angel most certainly would have been delighted to undertake Elijah's role, his task was to prepare Elijah to fulfill his divine calling.

At first glance, these verses appear mundane. Yet they are rich with practical significance for God's servants. We can learn much from this heavenly visitor about how to encourage someone who has grown weary and discouraged in God's service.

The angel *touched* him. Jezebel's desire to lay hands on Elijah was the original cause of his anxiety. But this touch was profoundly different. It was gentle, reassuring, and safe. The angel did not need to touch the prophet to awaken him. He could have shouted with the voice of a thousand trumpets. Perhaps the heavenly messenger understood Elijah's deep human need to be touched and cared for at that moment.

The angel provided *food* and *drink.* There are few aromas more delightful than that of bread baking! It is heavenly comfort food. The fact that bread was baking offers us a glimpse into Elijah's Master's loving concern. Did Elijah's meal need to be baked? Could it not have been dried, unleavened bread delivered by ravens? Could God not have provided fruit and seeds gathered from nearby plants? He most certainly could have. So why does God provide an angelic chef to build a fire and bake bread? Because God loves His servants! Why did Jesus cook fish for his disciples over an open fire after they fished all night and caught nothing? (John 21:5-12). He did so because He loved them. These feasts were not extravagant, but they were lovingly prepared and they provided comfort and strength. Oh that God's servants would be quick to recognize the gentle hand of their Master when He provides for them in timely, loving ways! God wasn't merely providing Elijah sustenance. He was letting His servant know He loved him.

The angel told Elijah to *rest.* This slumber was not intended as an escape, but as preparation. Elijah had a

200-mile walk ahead of him. The angel may also have understood that physical weariness directly affects our emotional and spiritual health. Taking a nap can radically transform our attitude! The angel knew better than to engage in a deep discussion with an exhausted servant. Such words would be wasted. Instead, the angel met the prophet's physical needs first so he would be prepared to have his spiritual needs addressed in time.

We should also note what the angel does not do. While he speaks words of instruction regarding Elijah's meals and rest, the angel does not discuss Elijah's circumstances. Most likely the angel knew God's plans for Elijah. Throughout the Bible, a word from an angel generally brought encouragement to hearers. But in this case, the angel speaks nothing about God's will for Elijah. He does not answer questions. He refuses to speculate about the future. He offers no condolences. The angel leaves the heart-to-heart discussion for God. There are times in people's lives when even a word from an angel is inadequate to alleviate the depth of their pain and discouragement. What is needed at such times is a word from almighty God. Longsuffering Job learned this lesson. Well meaning advice from friends or even angels can never replace one word from God. Elijah desperately needed a word from God. Nothing else would suffice.

The angel prepared Elijah for a forty-day sojourn to Sinai. After replenishing himself with food and drink, Elijah would embark on a 40-day fast in preparation for his encounter with God. Before his life-changing summit with the almighty, Elijah would spend forty days fasting in solitude. Much of Elijah's life was spent preparing for his next encounter with God.

This mountaintop event was the second in Elijah's life. The first had been on Mount Carmel, where he had experienced the pinnacle of his ministry. But now another mountain is called for. Elijah did not need another battlefield like Carmel, but a majestic meeting place like Sinai. The Israelites had been terrified by Mount Sinai when God settled upon it. Moses' encounter with God at Sinai was legendary:

> On the third day, when morning came, there was thunder and lightning, a thick cloud on the mountain, and a loud trumpet sound, so that all the people in the camp shuddered. Then Moses brought the people out of the camp to meet God, and they stood at the foot of the mountain. Mount Sinai was completely enveloped in smoke, because the Lord came down on it in fire. Its smoke went up like the smoke of a furnace, and the whole mountain shook violently. As the sound of the trumpet grew louder, Moses spoke and God answered him in the thunder (Ex. 19:16-19).

Elijah knew he must go to that mountain. Elijah needed a fresh encounter with almighty God. He had listened too long to people's voices. The confused prophet desperately needed a Mount Sinai experience. He longed to hear the voice of the God who originally called him into service.

Many people experience "burnout" at this point. They began their service strongly. They were zealous for their Lord and confident in their ability to serve Him. What they lacked in skill, they made up for with enthusiasm. But over time, wounds and disappointments take their toll. The call of God that once resounded so distinctly in their soul begins to grow distant and to lose its resonance. The love for God that once inspired enormous effort and sacrifice begins to wane. Sinai beckons the struggling servant, but the journey appears too distant and harsh. One delay after another sets in and before long, thoughts of returning to Sinai are set aside. There was a fountain of living water waiting at the mount, but the thirsty servant of God never found his way to it. Another casualty of the wilderness.

Fortunately for Elijah, heaven found him. An angel was dispatched. The resources of heaven were marshaled. God mobilized His forces so His servant would not be defeated or immobilized. As we read this account, we know in our hearts that God will do everything necessary to reclaim his discouraged servant. The question is not whether God can redeem a difficult situation, but whether God's servant will trust in God's provision. If Elijah chooses to remain where he is, all is lost. But if he arises and goes with God, exciting days still lie ahead. Though the journey ahead is long and arduous, the moment Elijah arises and sets his face toward Sinai, we know that another weary soul is on the brink of redemption. Having trusted God at his lowest point, Elijah commences a journey to his next divine encounter.

CONCLUSION

One of the most heartbreaking realities of God's kingdom is the countless men and women who grew weary and demoralized in their divine service. None of these dear people imagined they would ever arrive at such an abysmal place when they first set out following Jesus. But over time, they were wounded, deceived, and betrayed. Their focus shifted from their Savior to their troubles. The longer they listened to their critics, the more difficult it became to hear God's voice. Even the most devout followers of Christ can lose their way if they do not guard their heart and their relationship with their Lord. Yet Scripture is clear, there is no wilderness so vast or desolate or oppressive that the love of Christ cannot find us and lead us back to the mountaintop.

QUESTIONS TO CONSIDER

1. Are you currently walking intimately with your Lord? If you are not, what do you need to do to draw near to Him once more?

2. Is your physical or emotional condition affecting your spiritual condition? If so, what must you do?

3. Are you currently at a point of decision? Is there a choice you can make that will bring you out of the wilderness?

4. What are some of the practical, helpful ways God is currently expressing His love for you?

5. Have you been listening to the counsel of others who are concerned about you? Or, have you cut yourself off from those who want to help you?

CHAPTER SEVEN

Returning to the Heights

"He entered a cave there and spent the night. Then the word of the Lord came to him, 'What are you doing here, Elijah?'" (1 Kings 19:9)

1.A CLEFT IN THE ROCK

Elijah realized that if his ministry was to continue, he needed a fresh encounter with God. Elijah knew the stories of Moses' meeting with God at Sinai. Perhaps Elijah longed for a similar experience. So Elijah spent forty days traveling 200 miles through the wilderness.

The stakes were high. Elijah's entire future depended on his rendezvous with God.

Elijah entered a cave on the mount and waited for God. While we would expect Elijah to seek shelter on the mountain, we are left to speculate why he chose this particular cave. Centuries before, Moses had asked to see God's glory. He was frustrated with leading the rebellious Israelites. He needed a fresh vision of God. So he made the breathtaking request: *"Please, let me see Your glory"* (Ex. 33:18). The disloyal Israelites had continually complained. They even made a golden calf. Despite all God had done on their behalf, the people were reluctant to obey Him. If Moses were to continue working with such an obstinate, ungrateful people, he desperately needed a fresh vision of God. Such a request was unprecedented.

God responded by saying: *"'I will cause all of My goodness to pass in front of you, and I will proclaim the name Yahweh before you. I will be gracious to whom I will be gracious, and I will have compassion on whom I will have compassion.' But He answered, 'You cannot see My face, for no one can see Me and live'"* (Ex. 33:19-20). Moses sought more than he could handle. But God offered a compromise: *"Here is a place near me. You are to stand on the rock, and when My glory passes by, I will put you in the crevice of a rock and cover you with My hand until I have passed by. Then I will take My hand away, and you will see My back, but My face will not be seen"* (Ex. 33:21-23).

God knew His servant Moses needed to meet with Him. So He granted Moses as much of His presence as he could bear. But, to spare Moses' life, God placed him in a cleft of a rock. A cave. We have no way of knowing if the cleft God placed Moses in on Mount Sinai was the same cave Elijah would later inhabit. Perhaps Elijah searched the mountain for Moses' sacred meeting place. Or perhaps Elijah was instinctively drawn to the same kind of refuge God found for Moses. From our vantage point, we can only speculate.

We do know Elijah purposefully traveled 200 miles to the sacred mount. He fasted for forty days. Once he arrived at Sinai he was prepared to hear from his Lord. He was exhausted, discouraged, and afraid, but he was only one divine word away from a completely reinvigorated ministry.

2. DIVINE QUESTIONS

People ask their Maker countless questions. Why do the righteous suffer? Why do the wicked prosper? Why does Christ linger? Some of history's most brilliant thinkers agonized over such mysteries. Yet creation's most difficult questions are not those we present to God, but those God proffers to us.

Job insisted that if he could cross-examine God, he could prove his innocence (Job 13:15, 23). Suddenly the almighty responded: *"Who is this who obscures My counsel with ignorant words? Get ready to answer Me like a man . . ."* (Job 38:2-3). Then God began to ask

Job, *"Where were you?"* (Job 38:4). As God asked His questions, Job's confidence in his own righteousness vanished. By the time their conversation drew to a close, Job confessed: *"Surely I spoke about things I did not understand, things too wonderful for me to know"* (Job 42:3). God's questions completely unhinged the most righteous man on earth.

God's questions disarm and humble us. Questions such as, *"Where are you?"* (Gen. 3:9), *"Where is your brother . . .?"* (Gen. 4:9), *"What is that in your hand?"* (Ex. 4:2), *"Who should I send? Who will go for Us?"* (Is. 6:8), *"Is it right for you to be angry?"* (Jonah 4:4), *"But you . . . who do you say that I am?"* (Matt. 16:15), *"Saul, Saul, why are you persecuting Me?"* (Acts 9:4). Each time, God's question defined the encounter. People's queries faded into irrelevance. God's question brings the most important reality to the forefront. Once you have an answer to God's question, you also have the answer to yours.

So it was with Elijah. He waited for his meeting with God, brimming with queries for his Master. We can imagine what some of them may have been. Why had no one stood with him? Why had God done nothing about the evil Queen Jezebel? Why was his life still so difficult after years of faithful service? But Elijah never commenced his interrogation, for God spoke first. God didn't condemn His prophet. He didn't humiliate him or rebuke him. He simply asked a question.

"What are you doing here, Elijah?" (1 Kings 19:9). At first glance, this inquiry appears straightforward. It could almost be viewed as small talk. But God's words are never small. They always have a purpose. When God speaks, He lays people bare.

God is masterful in leading people to confess their condition. If people are ever to get to where God wants them to be, they must be willing to acknowledge where they are. Beginning with Adam and Eve, God has been asking, *"Where are you?"* (Gen. 3:9). Admitting where we are is disarming, liberating, and empowering. And where was Elijah at that moment? He was roughly 300 miles away from where God had last instructed him to go. Instead of standing triumphantly atop Mount Carmel, Elijah was in a darkened cave, by himself, on Mount Horeb. That was quite a contrast.

If God were to ask His servants the same question today, He would receive a wide array of answers. They might respond: "I am in a state of bitterness . . . I am estranged from my spouse . . . I am filled with anger . . . I am no longer a pastor . . . I am far from God . . ." If people were honest about their life, their answer to this question might reveal that they were no longer where God intended for them to be. Are you prepared for God's questions?

3. SELF-CENTERED DEPRESSION

"He replied, 'I have been very zealous for the Lord God of hosts, but the Israelites have abandoned

Your covenant, torn down Your altars, and killed
Your prophets with the sword. I alone am left, and
they are looking for me to take my life'" (1 Kings
19:10).

Elijah didn't like God's train of thought. God was
gently revealing that Elijah had abandoned his post
and was living in disobedience. Elijah did not want his
withdrawal to be the focus of their discussion. So he
changed the topic.

Elijah began by asserting his zeal for the Lord. Oh
the irony of the human heart! We can be hundreds of
miles from the post God assigned us and still believe we
are being faithful to Him! In this, Elijah was behaving
like King Saul. God told Saul to utterly obliterate the
Amalekites as an act of divine judgment (1 Sam. 15:1-3).
Saul defeated the Amalekites as he was commanded, but
then he disobeyed God's decree and spared the Amalekite
king and the best of the spoils. After disobeying God's
explicit instruction, Saul traveled from south of Judah
north to Mount Carmel to construct a monument to
commemorate his success! (1 Sam. 15:12). When Samuel
confronted the disobedient monarch, Saul declared:
"May the Lord bless you. I have carried out the Lord's
instructions." (1 Sam. 15:13). Samuel responded with
this unsettling question: *"Then what is this sound of*
sheep and cattle I hear?" (1 Sam. 15:14). One question
exposed Saul's sin and refuted Saul's declarations of
faithfulness.

Elijah earnestly declared his zeal for God, even while standing on Mount Horeb rather than Mount Carmel. Elijah attempted to shift the focus from his loyalty to his fellow Israelites' apostasy. *"But the Israelites have abandoned your covenant, torn down your altars, and killed your prophets with the sword"* (1 Kings 19:10). If God's servants cannot justify their own actions, they often try to blame others. Discussing the shortcomings of others is infinitely less troublesome than addressing our own sin. Just as King Saul ultimately blamed others for his disobedience (1 Sam. 15:15), Elijah attempted to justify his shortcomings by highlighting the failure of others.

We should not use others as a measuring stick for our faithfulness. Our obedience to God's will has nothing to do with other people. They cannot prevent us from being faithful. Only we can do that. Saul blamed his soldiers for his sin. Elijah blamed his fellow Israelites and Queen Jezebel for his desertion. Yet this justification was not, nor has it ever been, an acceptable excuse in God's eyes. Many ministers have declared, "I could not keep serving in my church when the people were acting as they were," as if the ungodly behavior of others prevented them from obeying what Christ told them to do. If Christ called you to a place of service, only He can call you away. Christ does not attach qualifiers to our call. He does not say, "Serve Me in this position. However, if people criticize your efforts, you are free to leave."

Christ fully understands obedience amid persecution. His enemies went so far as to kill Him in order to thwart God's plan. Yet even while hanging on a cruel cross, Jesus triumphantly declared, "It is finished!" Your enemies cannot prevent you from obeying God's will. Satan cannot stop you. Only you can scuttle God's will for your life.

Finally, Elijah got to the heart of the matter. *"I alone am left, and they are looking for me to take my life"* (1 Kings 19:10). Elijah was overcome with self-pity. Certainly we should refrain from casting stones upon someone who has a bounty on his head. But Elijah had lost his spiritual focus. As long as he kept his eyes on his Lord, Elijah saw his circumstances clearly. But the moment he shifted his attention to his problems, he became disoriented to the truth.

Notice Elijah's focus: *"The Israelites . . . they are looking for me . . . I alone . . ."* He mentioned his fellow citizens, his enemies, and himself. He never mentioned God. Elijah could not possibly know the truth of his situation without taking God into account.

His fellow citizens had indeed largely forsaken God. Jezebel was trying to kill him. But Elijah was not God's only remaining servant. Obadiah had preserved 150 of God's prophets, hiding them in groups of 50 while providing for their sustenance (1 Kings 18:3-4). Not only did God have a faithful servant embedded in a prominent government position, at least 150 devout prophets were in hiding. We also know that Elijah had dismissed his faithful servant only a few weeks previously (1 Kings 19:3). Clearly *feeling* alone does not mean you *are* alone.

Elijah may have felt as if he was the only prophet doing anything of consequence for the Lord. Everyone else was in hiding or incognito. God seemed to call on Elijah whenever He had an unpopular message for King Ahab. Such assignments caused Elijah to live in constant fear for his life. Elijah's self-pity magnified his own suffering and minimized the contributions of others. Certainly working closely with Ahab while risking his life every day caring for 150 prophets was not an easy calling for Obadiah. For that matter, it is challenging to subsist on bread and water while living in a cave, as the 150 prophets were doing. Elijah's complaint also minimizes the faithful service of his former servant who willingly followed him into the wilderness before Elijah abruptly dismissed him. Elijah was alone because he had cast off his only friend. The great prophet Elijah demonstrated how unattractive self-pity is, even when practiced by one of God's greatest servants.

Elijah had become disoriented to God. Such a condition is common for God's people. We take our eyes off Him, and soon our gaze is transfixed upon our enemies, our friends, our labors, our trials, or ourselves. God called Elijah during one of the darkest ages in Israel's history. He should have expected that, being called at midnight, he would inevitably confront darkness. But he grew weary. He became transfixed on the darkness and not on the Light that assigned him to his lampstand. Elijah talked as if everything revolved around him and that God should relieve him of his burdens. Elijah's story is a profound testimony and warning to how quickly we can descend from the mountaintop to a dark, lonely, bitter place. When God asked, *"What are you doing here,"* He exposed more than Elijah's address; He revealed Elijah's spiritual condition. For the prophet had become a bitter, self-pitying, lonely, weary man. Cleary Elijah was no longer useful to God until he refocused on his Lord and returned to the fellowship he once enjoyed. Fortunately for Elijah, he would soon learn that we are always just one divine encounter away from the greatest walk with God we have ever known.

CONCLUSION

There is an enormous difference between being God-centered and being self-centered. A person can be a Christian and still be entirely self-focused. Such people talk constantly about themselves. They worry about their problems. They bemoan their discomforts. They complain about how God manages their life. Not only does such behavior dishonor God, it debases the inherent nobility of that person.

God-centered people are not devoid of problems, pains, or persecutors. But they view them through the lens of their loving, all-powerful God. Their desire is not for their own vindication, but God's glory. They strive not for their will, but for God's will to be done. They count their own suffering and loss trivial compared to what their Savior sacrificed for them.

Though these contrasting behaviors appear to be worlds apart, they can occur in the same person. One day we live for the glory of God. The next day our heart shifts. As we watch Elijah call fire from heaven, we might doubt that he is in any way like us. But as we see him wallow in self-pity we realize that, indeed, he has a spirit just like ours (James 5:17). Let us plead for God to rescue us from ourselves before we slide hopelessly into the perilous abyss of self-pity.

QUESTIONS TO CONSIDER

1. Where do you go when you need a fresh encounter with God? Why does God do His best work in your life there?

2. What are the signs that you have lost your perspective in your service for God? What are the warning signs that you need a fresh encounter with God?

3. How do you avoid growing weary in your service for God? What are the signs you have become weary? What are the signs you have become self-focused?

4. Do you have a tendency to isolate yourself when you begin to struggle personally? How can you intentionally keep godly friends and counselors around you so you do not end up in a dark place?

5. Have you allowed your problems to blind you to the contributions and faithfulness of those around you?

CHAPTER EIGHT

Restored for Service

"Then He said, 'Go out and stand on the mountain in the Lord's presence.'" (1 Kings 19:11)

1.GO OUT AND STAND!

Elijah was wallowing in self-pity and discouragement. He wanted to quit. He had no hope for the future. Many of God's servants have been in a similar place. How do you help someone who sees nothing but darkness?

God's method of restoration is instructive. First, God's response did not address the points Elijah provided in his opening statement. Elijah wanted to discuss his past faithfulness, or the peoples' apostasy, or Jezebel's conspiracy. But when people are in a dark place, they generally do not see life clearly. As a result, they tend to focus on the wrong issues. God listened to Elijah and let him speak. But their discussion's focus would soon change. People in Elijah's condition should not prescribe their own remedy. God alone knows the pathway back to wholeness.

If you ask the wrong question, you will invariably obtain the wrong answer. God refused to engage in an unfruitful conversation. Instead, God commanded Elijah to leave the cave and stand in His presence. This instruction is interesting. Why vacate the cave in order to stand in God's presence? God is an expert conversationalist. He has conversed with people in the stomach of a fish (Jonah 2), in the stillness of the night (1 Sam. 3:10), and on rooftops (Acts 10:19-20). He certainly could have spoken to Elijah in a cave. Why does God reposition Elijah for his divine encounter? Why not speak with Elijah where He finds him?

Caves are dark places. From the inside, you can only see their narrow confines. You see no horizons. You view no sunrises. You discern no mountain peaks. You might reside in a cave at the top of Mount Everest, yet all you will see is a dark hole. Elijah suffered from a limited field of vision. He was on the same mountain that terrified the Israelites and where Moses' divine conversation left his face aglow, but all Elijah could see were dark, shadowy, stone walls. Perhaps his narrow perspective was why God told him to get up and leave the place he was dwelling.

Imagine the contrast when Elijah exited the gloomy cave and stood atop Mount Sinai. Suddenly he could view the majestic mountaintop. He could gaze over the expanse of the surrounding desert. He could see the glowing sun. He could detect the signs of life teeming about him. Simply by getting up and changing his venue, Elijah was already much better positioned to hear a word from God. Significantly, God did not move Elijah Himself. He told Elijah to get up and walk. Elijah could have chosen to remain in the dark cave that matched his mood. Or, he could trust his Lord, get up, leave the darkness, and step into the light.

This event tells us much about the power of perspective. Everything can seem bleak, dark, and hopeless. Yet we can move a few steps and suddenly be encircled with light and the warmth of sunshine. Scripture is filled with examples of discouraged people who discovered they were only a few divinely orchestrated steps away from an entirely new viewpoint.

2. A STILL, SMALL VOICE

"At that moment, the Lord passed by. A great and mighty wind was tearing at the mountains and was shattering cliffs before the Lord, but the Lord was not in the wind. After the wind there was an earthquake, but the Lord was not in the earthquake. After the earthquake there was a fire, but the Lord

was not in the fire. And after the fire there was a voice, a soft whisper" (1 Kings 19:11-12).

One word from God changes everything! God communicates with people in numerous ways. Biblically, however, the focus is never on God's method, but on His message. God chooses the means of guiding His servants that are best suited to their particular circumstances.

Elijah first encountered a great and mighty wind. The Holy Spirit is portrayed in Scripture as a wind (Acts 2:2). A mighty wind would certainly have been appropriate for Elijah. He needed a powerful outpouring of God's Spirit at this critical juncture in his life. But Scripture states that the Lord was not in the wind. A mighty wind cannot take the place of a mighty God! Clearly God makes use of various means to communicate with His servants. But the circumstances, no matter how magnificent, are meaningless unless God chooses to communicate through them.

After the wind was an earthquake. We would expect that when the Creator of the universe spoke, the earth would shake. In reality, when God speaks, His servants ought to quake. God once asked: *"Do you not tremble before Me?"* (Jer. 5:22). Nevertheless, God was not in the earthquake. God's voice is typically associated with thunder, lightning, and trumpets (Ex. 19:16), but He generally does not speak to His servants that way. While God is capable of overpowering people with His voice, He prefers to communicate in a manner that goes directly to their heart.

After the earthquake comes fire. God's word is often likened to a fire, for it is powerful and purifying. The prophet Jeremiah declared: *"If I say: I won't mention Him or speak any longer His name, His message becomes a fire burning in my heart, shut up in my bones."* (Jer. 20:9). God had recently answered Elijah's prayer with divine fire (1 Kings 18:38). Elijah may have assumed God would speak in the same manner again. But Elijah would learn that God is not confined to working with us in the same way He has before. God refuses to be reduced to a formula. While He never contradicts His written word, He is a God of surprises!

Perhaps God knew His prophet did not need another demonstration of fire. The last time God spoke through fire, 850 false prophets were violently executed and Elijah's enemies mobilized against him. God understood that His servant needed quiet, not tumult. The cacophony of shouts and sounds of conflict and destruction was not what Elijah's soul craved. The fire passed, but God was not in it.

Finally, Elijah detected a still, small voice. A soft whisper. *"When Elijah heard it, he wrapped his face in his mantle and went out and stood at the entrance of the cave"* (1 Kings 19:13). We might assume God's discouraged servant, overcome by fear, might require a dramatic display of power and might. Perhaps a combination of mighty wind, earthquake, and fire, as the children of Israel had once experienced at Sinai. We tend to associate God with the spectacular, with bright lights and loud noises. The danger in this assumption is that we strain to hear God in the spectacular and inadvertently overlook Him in the ordinary.

Elijah had already experienced the miraculous. He did not require another miracle, but an intimate relationship with his Creator. In the busyness of service, Elijah had taken his eyes off His Lord. He needed to return to the joy of his relationship so he could rejoice with David and exclaim: *"I love you, Lord, my strength. The Lord is my rock, my fortress, and my deliverer, my God, my mountain where I seek refuge, my shield and the horn of my salvation, my stronghold. I called to the Lord, who is worthy of praise, and I was saved from my enemies"* (Ps. 18:1-3).

In our day, weary, discouraged servants of God are commonplace. These frustrated people often assume they need a new job or a raise in pay or the removal of an antagonist. But the key is never a shift in circumstances, but a change in relationship. When we properly abide in our stronghold, it matters not who assails us. Our safety lies in entering into the fortress where our King offers His protection and comfort.

Once Elijah heard the gentle whisper of his Lord, he immediately recognized the speaker. Perhaps he learned to recognize God's whisper in the solitude of the wilderness or in the simplicity of the widow's cottage (1 Kings 17:3-7). Though people constantly look for the miraculous in their relationship with God, the most profound, life-changing encounters you may ever experience with the divine can occur in solitude as the Holy Spirit speaks directly to your soul. Elijah is best known for the epic events in his ministry. But what sustained him were quiet visitations with God. He had just experienced fire from heaven, yet he was ready to quit. After hearing God speak in a whisper, we have no record of Elijah ever wavering again.

3.DIVINE CONVERSATIONS

"Suddenly, a voice came to him and said, 'What are you doing here, Elijah?' 'I have been zealous for the Lord God of Hosts,' he replied, 'but the Israelites have abandoned Your covenant, torn down Your altars, and killed Your prophets with the sword. I alone am left, and they're looking for me to take my life'" (1 Kings 19:13-14).

Once again, God acted suddenly. Elijah was not startled by God's voice. By this time he was accustomed to the ways and timing of God. For Elijah, God's voice was sudden but not unexpected.

God asked the same question as before. What are you doing here? The first time God asked this, Elijah didn't answer; he made excuses. God refused to be sidetracked. When He repeated the question, Elijah responded by offering the identical excuse. Elijah's answer is verbatim to his initial response, as if he had rehearsed his answer and was staying on script. Of course, when we develop our reasoning in isolation, our arguments can seem compelling and irrefutable. Muttering to ourselves, we are convinced of our innocence and misfortune. But under heaven's cross-examination, our best defense comes tumbling down.

God welcomes our questions, but He never feels obligated to respond to our declarations. Elijah wanted God to confirm his analysis of the situation. Elijah kept trying to manage his conversation with God, but God refused to relinquish His role as Lord. As Lord, God directed their discussion. He was under no obligation to agree with Elijah's viewpoint or to answer his charges. God seeks to accomplish His own agenda in each discussion. Every divine word has a purpose. Divine silence can be deafening.

Elijah would have been better advised to make fewer statements and to ask more questions. He certainly could have asked God what He intended to do about Ahab and Jezebel. He could have asked what God's next assignment for him was. He could have asked God how He intended to bring revival to the land. Elijah might have asked many questions that would have provided clarity to his future. While pouring our hearts out to the Lord is often therapeutic, we don't typically learn anything new by doing so. We may feel better for having vented our frustrations, but our perspective remains flawed. We become wise when we bring our questions to God and receive His answers. Twice Elijah spewed out his frustrations and fears to God. God did not interrupt him, but neither did He answer him.

Prayer is a conversation. It is intended to be a two-way discussion between two unequal parties. While God welcomes our thoughts and concerns, God's words alone are transformative. Prayer is not intended for us to convince God to see our point of view or to alleviate the issues that trouble us. Rather, prayer is a divinely orchestrated experience where almighty God lays His heart over His servant's heart. It is how God enables us to view life from His perspective. It is how God moves us to care about what matters to Him. Elijah entered this prayer time eager to express his concerns to God. He left this encounter on mission with God. Such is the transformative nature of prayer.

CONCLUSION

Elijah found himself in an extremely dark, seemingly hopeless place. It might well have spelled the end of his successful ministry. His future clearly hung in the balance. Countless servants of God have found themselves in a similar condition. The temptation is to remain in the dark place, forfeit their divine calling, and spend the remainder of their life living in the shadows. Thankfully, Elijah allowed God to rescue him. He pulled himself out of the dark place where he was dwelling. He turned his attention from his own worries and fears to the God who was speaking. He kept listening until he finally discerned God's voice. His conversation with his Lord ultimately saved him. His enemies' threats and lies melted away as God's words filled his heart. God's words are not an additive to our life. They give us life. Listen carefully so you don't miss what almighty God is whispering to you.

QUESTIONS TO CONSIDER

1. Do you hear from God better when He shouts or when He whispers? Which has traditionally brought the most healing to your soul?

2. Do you ever find yourself in a dark cave? What has it required for you to escape the dark places in your life?

3. In your conversations with God, do you do more listening or talking? When you speak with God, do you tend to make declarations or ask questions? What was the last thing you clearly heard God say?

4. Do you try and maintain control of your conversations with God or do you follow His lead?

5. Are you spiritually weary? Do you need a fresh encounter with your Lord? Are you letting Him prepare you for a fresh encounter?

6. Do you tend to look for God in the dramatic? How good are you at recognizing God in the ordinary?

CHAPTER NINE

On Mission with God

"Then the Lord said to him, 'Go and return by the way you came to the Wilderness of Damascus'" (1 kings 19:15-16).

1. NEW ASSIGNMENTS

After praying fire down from heaven, what do you ask for next? What fresh challenge do you undertake? What new miracle do you ask God for? How do your dreams for the future change?

One of the most discouraging experiences God's servants suffer is when they suspect their best days are behind them. What if their major victories, accomplishments, and successes are in their past? People need to believe their life has a purpose. When we are young, our youthful vigor and imagination fosters optimism for the future. We look to the days ahead with eager anticipation. As time passes, our failures humble us. Enemies' attacks wound us. Disappointment by friends hardens us. It dawns on us that there are more years behind us than ahead of us. We may wonder if there is another significant challenge for us to undertake. Or, are we becoming increasingly archaic and irrelevant? Awakening each morning with nothing to inspire us is demoralizing.

Elijah felt tired and ready to die. He released his servant, assuming his ministry was over. Attacks and threats wore him down until he no longer felt capable of dealing with the constant troubles that beset him. Spiraling into a morass of self-pity and fear, Elijah could see nothing but a bleak future.

Notice God's response. First, God does not chastise Elijah. Though the fearful prophet had gone AWOL, his Lord did not condemn him. Nor did He threaten Elijah with dire consequences if he deserted again. God simply found and restored him. God focuses on the present, not the past (Is. 43:18-19). What we did yesterday matters far less than what we do today. We are never more than one step of obedience away from God's will.

God relates to us based on what He finds in our heart. Elijah's heart was heavy, but it was not sinful. Elijah did not have a track record of rebellion or disobedience. He had been faithful under extremely difficult circumstances. He had singularly taken a bold stand against evil. He was unlike Jonah, who deliberately fled in the opposite direction of where God commanded him to go. Elijah had fulfilled his mission on Mount Carmel. However, he had grown discouraged to learn that even fire from heaven was insufficient to bring revival to his land or to alleviate the constant attacks by his enemies. Elijah had done nothing morally wrong; he had simply lost heart.

Sadly, Elijah's situation describes many of God's servants today. Though the media tends to highlight ministers' moral failures, most people leave God's service because they grow weary and discouraged. Ironically, people who regularly preach about God's power and might are often the ones who grow discouraged themselves. Those who have witnessed the miraculous can lose hope for their own situation. People who have comforted others in the name of the Lord can become disheartened.

Second, notice that God does not enter into a prolonged debate or argument with His morose servant. God sees neither the need nor the value of such a discussion. Though we may be tempted to wallow in self-pity, God has no patience for it. Instead, God said, "go." God knows physical rest is crucial at times. But on other occasions, action and movement are therapeutic. God never responded to Elijah's complaints. Instead God commanded him to get on his feet and begin moving forward. When people are sitting still, they may feel as if they cannot take another step. Yet often the best way to regain our resolve is to take the first step in the right direction, regardless of whether we feel like it or not.

God told Elijah to return the same way he had come. He had to travel through the southern and northern kingdoms to reach Syria. His journey would be long. His situation is not uncommon. Often we find our way back into God's service by traveling down the same trail we took to depart from it. At times, God asks us to "remember" from where we have fallen (Rev. 2:5). By recalling where we once were with God, we can more easily retrace our steps to that place once more.

2. IMPACTING THE FUTURE

"'When you arrive, you are to anoint Hazael as king over Aram. You are to anoint Jehu son of Nimshi as king over Israel and Elisha son of Shaphat from Abel-meholah as prophet in your place'" (1 Kings 19:15).

Some people fixate on the past. They rehearse in their minds past failures, wounds, and disappointments. They recall criticism and unkind words. They speculate how their life would have been if only circumstances had unfolded differently. They squander countless hours focusing on a past they cannot change rather than on a future that is yet to unfold. When God speaks, there is always a future-orientation, because that is where He is leading us.

When you walk with God, there is always another chapter to your life. As long as you have breath, God intends to accomplish something through you. This reality reinvigorated Elijah. After raising someone from the dead, calling fire down from heaven, and ending a drought, Elijah might be excused for wanting to talk about days gone by. But incredibly, God did not discuss past events with His servant, because He had exciting new work awaiting him in the future.

God gave Elijah three major tasks. First, he was to anoint Hazael as king over Syria. This assignment was laden with significance. God instructed Elijah to anoint a future king. Clearly we are not always the best judges of our future possibilities. Elijah wanted to resign, despairing of his future prospects. God told him he would anoint kings and determine the fate of nations. Hazael was not just any king. He was the ruler of Syria. He and his people were God's enemies. In fact, Hazael was an ancient terrorist. His people would inflict all manner of horrors on the Israelites (2 Kings 8:12). God was making an enormous statement. He was declaring that He is not only sovereign over His own people, but over every nation on earth. God was even sovereign over the most evil, murderous terrorists in the ancient world. God can use any person He chooses to accomplish His purposes.

Second, God told Elijah to anoint Jehu as king over Israel. This, too, seems unusual. Elijah had been in hiding from Ahab and Jezebel because they wanted to kill him.

Now Elijah learned he would anoint their replacements. Elijah may have wondered why a righteous God tolerated evil government leaders such as these. Then he learned that God intended to judge them. We should never worry that someone will avoid the divine punishment due them. God is absolutely righteous. Though He may show patience to even the most abominable sinner, God will eventually hold everyone accountable for their every word, thought, and deed (2 Cor. 5:10). Though Elijah suffered while Ahab ruled the land, God reminded Elijah of the terrible truth that *"It is a terrifying thing to fall into the hands of the living God!"* (Heb. 10:31).

Elijah had also wondered if his life and ministry made any difference in his nation. Despite his preaching and miracles, evil was widespread. But God alerted Elijah that he would anoint his nation's next king. Alone, Elijah had minimal influence. In God's hand, Elijah raised up kings.

Finally, God instructed Elijah to anoint Elisha as his replacement. This moment was poignant for Elijah. Elijah was the greatest prophet of his day, yet he was not indispensable. He performed miracles in God's name, but Elisha would accomplish even more. Elijah is clearly the servant and God is the Master. Elijah was not allowed to quit on his terms. Neither did he choose his successor. God's work is greater than any one person, regardless of their stature, skills, or saintliness.

One of the greatest privileges God grants His servants is the opportunity to touch the future. Humanity's life span is exceedingly brief (Ps. 39:5). The journey from infant to senior citizen is alarmingly rapid. Soon the strength and vigor of youth gives way to declining health and eventually death. No one, not even the most powerful, can avoid this destiny. Yet some people are given the enormous invitation to touch the future. By investing in the next generation, they influence what that generation becomes.

Elijah was tempted to behave as many aging leaders do and retire from the field, complaining about the sorry state of the nation. At a time when Elijah had more to contribute than ever before, he had intended to withdraw into solitude. Instead, God granted him the greatest assignments of his life. His actions would lead to two kings ascending the throne and his own worthy successor rising up to take his place. Elijah wanted to quit. Instead, God granted him the exhilarating opportunity to impact generations to come.

3. GOD'S JUDGMENT

"Then Jehu will put to death whoever escapes the sword of Hazael, and Elisha will put to death whoever escapes the sword of Jehu. But I will leave 7,000 in Israel—every knee that has not bowed to Baal and every mouth that has not kissed him" (1 Kings 19:17-18)

Some of the most oft-asked questions concerning God are these: Why does God allow evil people to prosper? Why does He allow people, especially good people, to suffer? This seeming injustice may have been part of Elijah's dilemma. He had been forced to live as an enemy of the state because evil people led the nation. Many of the government and religious leaders were corrupt and inflicted much suffering on God's people. After working for years to bring about national revival, Elijah finally gave up and resigned his prophetic office.

Ultimately, Elijah learned the extent of both God's grace and justice. By His grace, God granted ample time for His people to return to Him. God even demonstrated abundant grace toward king Ahab. Scripture declares: *"Still there was no one like Ahab, who devoted himself to do what was evil in the Lord's sight, because his wife Jezebel incited him. He committed the most detestable acts by going after idols as the Amorites had, whom the Lord had dispossessed before the Israelites"* (1 Kings 21:25-26). Surely Ahab deserved to receive the full measure of God's wrath. Nevertheless, God granted Ahab access to the greatest prophet in his nation's history. God also provided Ahab the righteous prophet Micaiah, who always told him God's truth (1 Kings 22:6-28). God showed mercy to Ahab when he humbled himself (1 Kings 21:27-29). It seems incredible that God would tolerate an evil king like Ahab for as long as He did. Why not strike down the insolent monarch? Yet God repeatedly showed him grace rather than judgment. Ironically, by being longsuffering toward Ahab, God caused Elijah to endure constant danger and opposition. God's grace to one person resulted in suffering for another.

The apostle Peter assured us God is not slow to act (2 Peter 3:9). However, God often moves more methodically than we might expect against evil people, granting them time to repent. Eventually, people reject God's grace and God's wrath is assured. Now Elijah understood the magnitude of God's impending judgment. King Hazael would inflict grievous suffering on the Israelites. God would use a pagan terrorist to judge His people. Though Hazael might mock the Israelites' God, he was, in reality, merely a divine instrument. The people of Elijah's day vaguely understood how God worked among the nations. They believed each nation had its own deity. The most powerful nation clearly had the greatest god. The Israelites knew the Syrians served a false god, yet they would have been surprised to learn that the true God was orchestrating events among pagan nations. Rather than wondering why the Syrians were so cruel, God's people should have considered what offense they had committed that motivated God to use the Syrians to punish them.

Those Israelites who survived Hazael's sword would suffer Jehu's wrath. Once again, God's ways challenge our sensibilities. Jehu was an unsavory character. His reign was permeated with bloodshed. He murdered King Joram of Israel and King Ahaziah of Judah (2 Kings 9:24-28). He also had Jezebel murdered (2 Kings 9:30-37). He had 70 sons of Ahab beheaded (2 Kings 10:1-11) and 42 brothers of Ahaziah executed (2 Kings 10:12-114). Jehu instructed his soldiers to massacre a large gathering of pagan priests (2 Kings 10:18-28).

Jehu mercilessly purged Israel of any relative, friend, or lieutenant of Ahab, as well as any priest of Baal.

What made Jehu particularly repugnant was that, not only was he a murderous insurgent, he also worshiped golden calves originally established by the evil king Jeroboam (2 Kings 10:29-31). Jehu was an idolater, and yet God used him to bring judgment on others. Let us never say that God cannot use an "unclean vessel." For God surely used Jehu to judge Israel, just as He used the Assyrians, King Nebuchadnezzar, and the Roman legions. These invaders did not know they were God's servants, but that did not prevent God from using them.

Certainly God prefers to use holy vessels. But at times, the very fact that God raises up particularly despicable individuals as leaders may itself be a means of divine judgment. While we can generally recognize God's hand when He uses a godly servant to carry out His will, recognizing God's hand when He uses ungodly people to perform His work takes greater spiritual discernment.

As God revealed His will to His servant, Elijah began to understand what was happening in his nation. Ahab and Jezebel would not escape God's judgment. The Israelites who had forsaken the true God would not go unpunished. In fact, their suffering would be extreme. God was working out His purposes in His time and in His way, but God's justice would be certain and terrifyingly thorough. No righteous act would go unrewarded and no sinful deed would be exempt from justice.

God mentioned something almost as an aside. He still had 7,000 servants who had not compromised their faith. Earlier, Elijah bemoaned the fact that he was the only servant God had left (1 Kings 19:10, 14). God did not argue with him at the time, but now God made it clear that Elijah did not understand the situation as well as he thought. God had many faithful servants at His disposal. They did not all have the prominent assignment Elijah had, but God had access to them as He accomplished His purposes. Elijah mistakenly assumed that if others were not engaged in the same activity he was then they were not faithfully serving the Lord. Elijah had been too quick to judge his brethren.

Why do God's servants need to abide in Christ? Because as they walk closely with the Lord, they recognize how God is building up His kingdom through servants such as Elisha. They will also discern how God is bringing judgment on the land through ungodly instruments such as Hazael and Jehu. When God's people abide in Christ, the national and international events of their day will not bewilder them.

4. RETURNING TO THE MISSION

"Elijah left there and found Elisha son of Shaphat as he was plowing. Twelve teams of oxen were in front of him, and he was with the twelfth team. Elijah walked by him and threw his mantle over him. Elisha left the oxen, ran to follow Elijah, and said, 'Please let me kiss my father and mother, and

then I will follow you.' 'Go on back,' he replied, 'for what have I done for you?' So he turned back from following him, took the team of oxen, and slaughtered them. With the oxen's wooden yoke and plow, he cooked the meat and gave it to the people, and they ate. Then he left, followed Elijah, and served him." (1 Kings 19:19-21).

We find encouragement from the simple phrase, *"Elijah left there"* (1 Kings 19:19). It appeared for a time that he might never depart from the wilderness, but choose instead to live out his remaining days suffering from fear and discouragement. Then upon his arrival at Sinai, we would not have been surprised had he chosen to spend his final days in solitude on the mountaintop enjoying blissful communion with his Lord. What becomes clear is this: the wilderness and the mountaintop have unique roles to play in the life of God's servants, but they are not intended to be a final destination. They are places of preparation, healing, and restoration but not retirement.

Our heart exults to read that Elijah chose to leave Mount Horeb and return to God's service. Elijah had waged battle with dark forces in his soul and he had vanquished them. Mount Horeb would not become a graveyard for his ministry but a place of renewal.

When we were first introduced to Elijah, he was a preacher, speaking to kings and announcing a devastating drought. His subsequent ministry took many twists and turns. He had finally come full circle. Rather than building his career, he mentored his successor. Seeing our ministry grow and expand can be exhilarating. But a unique joy results from investing in young people and watching their walk with God mature and prosper.

Once Elijah was again on mission with God, he wasted no time finding Elisha. Elisha was a farmer. We assume his father, Shaphat, needed him to provide labor for the family business. We know nothing of Elisha's education or pedigree. What Scripture does reveal is that he was physically strong and he was full of enthusiasm. While physical strength is rarely a prerequisite for serving God, passion is. God delights in finding people who are enthusiastic about serving Him. Elijah had been discouraged and wanted to quit. Then we are introduced to Elisha. When he was invited to join Elijah, he kissed his mother and father goodbye, slaughtered a pair of oxen, burned their yoke, and threw a farewell party. He would not look back! The contrast between the veteran prophet and this farm boy is profound. Elijah had grown weary in serving. Elisha could hardly be constrained! Elijah had become cynical. Elisha abounded with optimism. While training his zealous disciple, Elijah became refreshed for service. God's work is too extensive for any one person or church, regardless of how great they might be. After Elijah left, Elisha remained. And when Elisha breathed his last, God's work continued. In communing with God, Elijah saw his role clearly and embraced it fully. Such has been the history of Christendom.

CONCLUSION

Elijah may best be known for two things: calling down
fire from heaven on Mount Carmel and being carried to
heaven by a chariot of fire. How glorious service for God
would be if it always involved spectacular events such as
these. Yet the key to Elijah's great success lies not in the
fire and the mountaintops, but in the "in between times."
Elijah's spiritual power and authority stemmed from his
personal and dynamic relationship with his Lord.

Elijah would never have preached such a devastating
message to his nation had he not been communing with
God. He certainly could not have survived a wilderness
or a drought in Zaraphath had he not learned to walk
by faith with the almighty. Had God not deepened his
prayer life, Elijah could never have witnessed the dead
restored to life. Certainly the dramatic showdown on
Mount Carmel was a defining moment in Elijah's life, but
it only occurred because of the years he spent faithfully
walking with his Lord in the difficult places. Elijah's
ministry might well have come to a premature end after
Mount Carmel had his walk with God not been restored
atop Mount Horeb.

Whether God was preparing Elijah to perform
miracles, or teaching Elijah to trust Him for the
impossible, or restoring his faith in times of trials and
opposition, the key to Elijah's ministry was God. What
made Elijah unique was that he continually drew near to
his Lord and trusted Him, regardless of his circumstances.
When Elijah's faith wavered, he walked 200 miles and

fasted for forty days in order to experience God afresh. He demonstrated the profound truth that when we draw near to God, He will draw near to us (James 4:8).

The apostle James assured us that Elijah was a person just like us (James 5:17). More importantly, Elijah's God is the exact same God as our God. To make matters even more poignant, the current condition of our society appears very much like that of Elijah's time. God is seeking people today who will allow Him to work in their lives just as he did with Elijah. Many people today long for the power of Elijah, but far fewer are prepared to pay the price of Elijah. Oh that you would be such a one!

QUESTIONS TO CONSIDER

1. What has God revealed to you through your walk with Him about what is happening in your life, in your church, in your family, and in your nation?

2. Do you need to return to a place you once were with Christ? Do you need to retrace your steps?

3. How are you currently investing in the future? How are you blessing in the next generation?

4. How might God want to use your life to impact your nation or the world?

5. Where do you see God bringing judgment on sin?

6. Do you need spiritual renewal? If you do, what is God currently doing to bring that about?

Moses: Pursuing God's Vision

INTRODUCTION

Great dreams motivate great lives. People need a grand purpose for their existence, for life is too precious to spend cheaply. Advancing God's kingdom is the noblest cause to which people can devote their solitary life. As God sweeps people up into His eternal purposes, He inspires them to live fully and passionately for His glory.

The apostle Paul declared that he was driven by a heavenly vision (Acts 26:19). Isaac, Samuel, Samson, and John the Baptist knew God had ordained their life with a divine purpose. As a teenager, Jeremiah learned that God had a unique calling on his life (Jer. 1:5). David understood that, before he was born, God knew him and had breathtaking plans for him (Ps. 139:16). Noah spent many years pursuing his life's calling. Nehemiah, Esther, and Mary discovered God had an assignment for them that would define their life. The profound vision of becoming fishers of men compelled Peter, Andrew, James, and John to abandon their fishing business. Men and women who embraced heaven's vision for their life have been plunged into the midst of God's timeless activity to transform their world.

Some people struggle for years to find their life's purpose. Without a dream or vision, they meander aimlessly through life searching for fulfillment. Others, like Samson and Jonah, know God's will but resist it, often bringing calamity on themselves and others. Still other individuals, like Joseph, Joshua, and Nehemiah, strive to accomplish God's purposes but encounter numerous hardships, enemies, and disappointments en route.

What makes Moses so fascinating is his vacillating approach to his calling. At times Moses enthusiastically embraced God's vision. Other times he rejected it. Sometimes he overcame major opposition to stay on course. At moments the heavenly vision appeared to be almost within his grasp. On other occasions it seemed hopelessly distant. When Moses was young, he energetically gripped God's dream for his life. However, in his youthful zeal, Moses attempted to fulfill the heavenly vision in his own strength rather than God's. The result was dismal failure. For forty years Moses' dream appeared to be buried in the sands of Egypt along with the oppressive Egyptian taskmaster. Then, to Moses' surprise, God found him in the wilderness and announced that his life's calling had never been revoked. Then, his self-confidence eviscerated, Moses resisted the dream. He viewed himself as too unskilled to accomplish what he had envisioned doing in his youth. Moses eventually surrendered to the heavenly vision. However, Pharaoh stood stubbornly in the way. Only God's miraculous intervention enabled the Israelite's liberation. Once out of Egypt, Moses' dream was imperiled once again. The sin and unbelief of his own people derailed his plans. He spent forty more years waiting for the moment he could advance toward the goal God originally set before him.

Dreams are precarious. They are always just one foolish act away from crashing upon the rocks. You cannot live casually, immorally, or unethically and achieve God's vision for your life. One illegal act, one adulterous dalliance, one angry outburst and your future can change dramatically. Countless people have forfeited God's dream for their life because they became careless, casual, or conceited.

Two realities produce a sense of urgency for heavenly dreams. The first involves the stakes. Others suffer when we fail to embrace God's purposes for our life. In Moses' case, an entire nation desperately longed for freedom. They languished in bondage for generations. While Moses argued with God in the wilderness about whether or not he had the necessary qualifications to do what God intended, thousands of people suffered. The second reality involves our age. When we are young, we assume we have adequate time to achieve God's purposes for our life. But as we grow older, we become aware that time is passing and so are our opportunities. As our strength fades, we recognize that if we do not achieve God's vision for our lives soon, we never will. Such was the case with Moses.

Moses' life is treated extensively in the Old Testament, so we know his story well. He was a spiritual giant who cast a long shadow over Scripture. Rather than tracing his story from a baby miraculously rescued from the Nile River to his unusual burial on Mount Nebo, we will examine Moses' final days as a leader.

What does finishing well look like? And, why do so many of God's servants fail to do so? While the way we begin a race is crucial, how we end it is far more important. We expect aging saints to be paragons of faith and holiness. We trust such people to finish well. Tragically, this hope is not always justified. Such was the case with Moses.

CHAPTER TEN

Holding on to the Dream

"The entire Israelite community entered the Wilderness of Zin in the first month, and they settled in Kadesh" (Numbers 20:1)

1. REMEMBERING THE DREAM

Some comments in Scripture nearly escape our notice. They appear to be mundane details we must read before arriving at the important theological truths awaiting us deeper in the text. The Israelites had broken camp and relocated short distances countless times throughout the years. This verse appears to be simply another journal entry in Moses' travel diary. But this move is enormously significant.

Because they failed to believe God could grant them victory over the Canaanites, the Israelites spent four decades enduring a gradual death sentence. They were experiencing daily the sobering truth that, without faith, it is impossible to please God (Heb. 11:6). God punished the unbelievers by making them exist only a stone's throw from the land of their dreams. God's judgment was final. He did not negotiate or make amendments. The Israelites' dream to live in a land flowing with milk and honey would die with them in the desert. So, day-by-day, year-by-year, decade-by-decade, the people waited to die. Because they had forfeited God's vision for them, they existed but did not truly live.

When we arrive at Numbers 20, a significant shift occurs. By this time, the generation of unbelieving adults has passed from the scene. Their children had become adults. These young people were forced to grow up in a wilderness, not because of their own unbelief, but because of their parent's faithlessness. The younger generation experienced first hand the grim reality that when parents fail to trust God and His word, their loved ones suffer. These people should have spent their childhood growing up in a land flowing with milk and honey. Instead, they spent their youth collecting manna each morning in the desert.

This Scripture marks a turning point. God finally commenced the process of leading them into the Promised

Land. Their parents squandered their opportunity. At last it was the next generation's turn.

After living forty years in a desert, the Israelites might well have assumed their dream of living in the Promised Land would never become a reality. After all, their parents had witnessed God levy ten devastating plagues upon Egypt and reduce it to its knees. They experienced God part the Red Sea, then swallow the Egyptian army within its depths. They were terrified at the foot of Mount Sinai as almighty God descended upon it. Yet for all God's spectacular displays of might, the Israelites assumed God was unable to give them the Promised Land. Fierce, giant-like peoples resided in impregnable walled cities throughout the land. The Israelites had been so frightened by what they saw that they wept uncontrollably and begged to return to Egypt as slaves (Num. 14:1-4).

Those adults died and their children now stood in their place. God graciously offered the same vision to them. Would they trust Him to provide a land flowing with milk and honey? The dream had not died! It had only been delayed. God had not forgotten His promise. He had simply waited for someone to believe Him for it.

Untold numbers of God's servants have assumed the dream God gave them as a youth had long since expired. After many years, the vision that inspired them as young adults appeared naïve, almost ludicrous. But what an amazing moment it is to learn that God has not forgotten

His promises of years gone by. He remains prepared to accomplish them through our life if only we will believe.

Imagine the excitement that rippled through the Israelite camp when they realized God was marching them toward Canaan! Their lives would not be filled with purposeless wandering. Consider what raced through Moses' heart and mind. Entering the Promised Land was his life's dream. We assume that when he was a child his parents and sister Miriam told him how he was miraculously rescued as a baby and how God had a special purpose for his life. He had spent forty years herding sheep in the wilderness, wondering if his dreams were lost. Then he spent another forty years in the wilderness because of his people's unbelief. At 120 years old, Moses naturally assumed his greatest days of divine service had passed him by. Then, suddenly, God instructed him to break camp and advance toward the Promised Land! That day must have been one of the most joyful of Moses' life. Yet, as we know, drawing close to the Promised Land is not the same as entering it.

2.LIFE'S CHOICES

Life consists of a series of choices. How we respond to those decisions sets the direction of our life. A series of wise choices can take a person far down the road to success. One foolish decision can derail the journey.

Moses suffered for most of his life due to a handful of unwise decisions. He was not characteristically foolish, but his life hinged on certain watershed moments. Our life typically progresses the same way. Though we make many small, mundane decisions throughout our life, we could likely trace the overall success or failure of our life to only a handful of major decisions. In Moses' case, he usually acted wisely, but occasionally he committed colossal blunders. Unfortunately, one foolish decision can negate years of wise living.

Moses' flawed decisions typically occurred when he acted out of anger. Although the Bible doesn't specifically tell us Moses was angry when he struck down the Egyptian, we may assume he did so in wrath (Ex. 2:11-12). That incident cost him forty years herding sheep. When the Israelites made a golden calf, *"Moses became enraged and threw the tablets out of his hands, smashing them at the base of the mountain"* (Ex. 32:19). That act of anger cost Moses another trip up the mount to obtain replacements (Ex. 34:1-4). Scripture reveals several occasions when the Israelites angered him (Ex. 16:20; 32:19; Num. 16:15). Nevertheless, on many occasions he maintained his self-mastery while dealing with disappointment and opposition (Num. 12:1-3; 14:5). Moses would learn that years of faithfulness are undone by brief ungodly moments.

Though Moses dreamed of entering the Promised Land all his life, he will commit an act that will forever close the door to what he most wanted. The following verses will show the greatest blunder in Moses' life. And if a man who talked with God face to face could make such a costly mistake, we are certainly vulnerable of doing the same thing ourselves.

3. RETURNING TO KADESH

God's ways are not our ways (Is. 55:8-9). His manner of working in people's lives is rigorously consistent with His nature. God takes no shortcuts to godliness. He makes no allowance for faithlessness. He accepts no substitute for obedience. Nevertheless, God repeatedly catches us by surprise.

After mobilizing the people, the first thing God did was lead them to Kadesh. It is somewhat surprising that the first place God leads the Israelites as they approach the Promised Land is to the site of their failure of faith 40 years earlier. It was at Kadesh that the children of Israel concluded it was impossible to conquer the land. Surely there must have been a less intimidating entry point to Canaan. Why not make the journey easier on the Israelites this time so they were more likely to succeed?

But God was not going to allow their prior setback to continue to define them. Kadesh had loudly proclaimed that the Israelites were cowards and failures. God would remove that epitaph from His people and write a new story. God was determined to transform the Israelites from a people of defeat to a people of victory.

We generally recognize points of weakness in our life. In response, we tend to avoid those areas lest we suffer additional setbacks. We prefer to concentrate on our strengths and avoid our weaknesses. But God does not work that way. Before God led His people onward to fresh victories, He made them address their previous failure.

4. LOSING MIRIAM

"Miriam died and was buried there" (Num. 20:1)

We come to a seemingly minor point in the narrative. Moses' older sister Miriam died. The text mentions this event briefly, almost as an afterthought. Her passing is inserted between the announcement of the Israelites breaking camp and an account of the Israelites complaining about a lack of water. In the grand scheme of events, we might not expect that the passing of a woman of more than 120 years would garner much notice. However, Miriam had a special place in Moses' life. She was the one who watched over his little ark of bulrushes on the Nile while he was hiding from the Egyptian butchers (Ex. 2:3-4). When Pharaoh's daughter discovered the baby, Miriam approached her and offered to find a nurse for the infant. Such aplomb not only saved Moses' life, it also enabled him to grow up in the royal court.

Miriam was a prophetess, which means she received words from God and delivered them to the people (Ex. 15:20). She was also a singer and worship leader (Ex. 15:20-21). She was not sinless (Num. 12:1-16), but the Israelites regarded her highly (Micah 6:4). Then she died. Not many women's deaths are recorded in the Bible. We are not told when Moses' wife Zipporah died. But Miriam is mentioned because of her stature among the people.

Moses may well have recorded her death because he viewed it as a significant personal loss. Not only did her passing remind Moses of his own mortality, it also caused him to lose one of his only remaining advisors. Moses was not particularly gifted at working with others. However, a few people, like his father-in-law Jethro, were able to speak words of wisdom to him. Jethro had presumably died many years earlier. Now his loyal sister Miriam had departed as well.

We can only speculate at this point, but it is significant that Moses made the worst mistake of his life soon after losing one of his most trusted supporters. We should never underestimate the impact that losing a friend or supporter has on us. Moses did not act with his typical humility in this account. He had previously weathered numerous storms and maintained his meek trust in God. However, Moses would succumb to his emotions in the coming trial and behave uncharacteristically. Leaders often assume their personal life has no impact on their leadership. But leaders who have recently suffered a personal loss or disappointment may be unusually vulnerable when attempting a major undertaking.

The stage was set for one of the most dramatic encounters and excruciating failures in Moses' long life. The people were advancing once more toward the Promised Land. They had returned to the place of their previous failure. Moses' sister and trusted messenger of God had died. Strong emotions surely raced through Moses' heart. His lifelong dream finally loomed on the horizon. Yet dreams are not grasped easily. Life is rarely devoid of challenges. Success or failure can hinge on just one moment or decision.

CONCLUSION

Our life has a context. We do not walk with God in a vacuum. While we wish we could serve God under ideal conditions, life rarely affords such a luxury. Inevitably we find ourselves arriving at our own Kadesh. Such places represent a messy, unpredictable, complicated world. Yet, though we may not be able to choose our Kadesh, we are always free to select our response to it. We can either grow discouraged by the difficulties we face, or we can allow God to guide us through a maze of complex issues and circumstances so our life becomes an instrument to accomplish His divine purposes. The more difficult our situation, the greater the opportunity to glorify God! Don't spend your life trying to avoid Kadesh. Rather, diligently prepare yourself so when you arrive at it, you are fully prepared to honor God by your response.

QUESTIONS TO CONSIDER

1. Has God planted a dream in your heart? If so, what is it?

2. Have you accomplished your life's dream, or does it appear to be impossibly far away?

3. Is there a failure in your life you have never properly processed and achieved victory over? Is God trying to take you back there?

4. Have you lost a trusted friend, team member, or supporter recently? If so, how has that affected you?

5. Are you currently in a condition personally where you are spiritually, emotionally, or relationally unprepared for God to do a great work in and through our life?

CHAPTER ELEVEN

Enemies of the Dream

"There was no water for the community, so they assembled against Moses and Aaron." (Num. 20:2)

1. BARREN DESTINATIONS

It can be confusing when a loving, omniscient God leads us to unpleasant places. God is infinitely wise and perfectly loving. Nonetheless, in order to accomplish His purposes in our life, God may guide us into difficult circumstances. When He does, we might be tempted to question whether God has made a mistake or if He truly loves us.

Once God began leading the Israelites toward Canaan, the first place He took them was Kadesh. Not only was Kadesh where the children of Israel experienced their most dismal failure, it was also devoid of water. God's plan once again befuddled the Israelites. Since Kadesh was where the Israelites had lost heart before, we might assume God would make the experience more palatable for His people this time. Surely He did not want them to fail a second time. We could imagine God lining the path with oases brimming with fruit and water to prepare the Israelites for the rigorous invasion awaiting them. But such was not the case.

Instead, the first thing God did once He mobilized His people was lead them directly to a desolate place in the desert. Why would He do this? From a military vantage point, this decision appears to signify poor leadership. Astute generals do not intentionally lead an invading army to camp at a location without water. Doing so invites disaster.

Many of God's servants have had similar experiences. They felt God leading them to serve in a particular church or ministry or to take on a new job. Upon their arrival, they were met with criticism and opposition. Bewildered, they questioned whether they had heard God correctly. They cannot fathom why a loving God would lead them to a unpleasant place.

When we face difficult circumstances, we must carefully consider the ways of God. God's ways focus not on producing minimum discomfort for us, but bringing maximum glory to Him. If our life can bring God greater glory by enduring trials, we must expect God to regularly take us to such places. In addition, God is always more concerned with who we are than what we do. The Israelites were focused on entering the Promised Land. But God knew they were unprepared to do so. So God led them directly to a faith-building experience. He was testing them. Could it be that after forty years of walking with God, the Israelites still had a surface knowledge of Him and a shallow faith? The people assumed they were prepared to take on giants in Canaan. But in truth, they were not even ready to face thirst at Kadesh.

Trials do not make or break us. They expose us. God laid bare the Israelites' flaws and weaknesses at the start of their journey rather than in the heat of battle. One of the most dangerous experiences to afflict God's servants is early success. When we initially succeed in our efforts, we can assume we have nothing more to learn. Conversely, early failure humbles us and compels us to prepare for the future. God provided the Israelites with a test of character before they undertook the greatest challenge of their lives. The result was as enlightening as it was disappointing.

2. DREAM CRITICS

". . . so they assembled against Moses and Aaron. The people quarreled with Moses and said, 'If only we had perished when our brothers perished before the Lord. Why have you brought the Lord's assembly into this wilderness for us and our livestock to die here?'" (Num. 20:2-4)

These words deeply affected Moses. They were eerily similar to what he heard forty years earlier (Num. 14:1-4). At that moment, Moses faced a stark realization. He had waited forty years for the complaining, unbelieving opponents to his leadership to die so he could finally lead a faithful people into the Promised Land. Yet after the unbelieving generation of Israelites expired, Moses discovered to his great dismay that the next generation was no better than the last. Moses had waited forty years to outlast the complainers, but they had outlasted him!

Many Christian leaders have shared Moses' dismal experience. Pastors grew tired of the constant complaints and attacks they suffered from their congregation, so they finally accepted a call to another church. However, after relocating to a new post, they discovered complaining, critical members in their new congregation as well. Leaders who long for uncomplaining followers are destined for disappointment. Of one thing leaders can be certain: regardless of how great the leader or how noble the task, some people will always complain.

The perplexing question is why the next generation grumbled. These people had spent 40 years wandering aimlessly in the wilderness as a result of their parents' refusal to trust God. Surely a 40-year lesson on the consequences of unbelief ought to have thoroughly purged the younger generation of their doubts and fears! Yet at the first opportunity to demonstrate their superior faith, the next generation succumbed to grumbling and complaining as well.

One of the tragic ironies of the human condition is that, regardless of how appalled we may be by our parents' behavior, we instinctively look to them as our primary role models. Why did the younger generation become grumblers and complainers? They grew up in homes of grumblers and complainers. Why did they become fearful adults? Because they were reared in homes dominated by fear. Being exposed to continual complaints inevitably exerts a debilitating effect. Despite knowing full well the consequences of their parents' lack of faith, the children grew up to embrace identical sins and shortcomings.

Most people are oblivious to how powerfully their role models affect them. Frugal parents spawn miserly children. Lazy parents rear indolent offspring. Obese parents bring up overweight children. Spiritually shallow parents produce spiritual infants. One reason parents should strive for maturity in their Christian life should be so they do not predispose their children to suffer the same spiritual mediocrity and failure as their parents.

3.PROMISES AND LIES

"'Why have you led us up from Egypt to bring us to this evil place? It is not a place of grain, figs, vines, and pomegranates, and there is no water to drink!'" (Num. 20:5).

Satan is the father of lies (John 8:44). His most sinister weapon is deception. If he can distort people's view of reality, he will enslave them. Adam and Eve believed a lie and it cost them paradise. The Israelites accepted a lie and it cost them the Promised Land. Every time Christians advance, they must do two things. First, they must embrace a truth of God. Second, they must renounce a lie of Satan (John 8:32). Inevitably, when Christians experience defeat, discouragement, or spiritual decline, they have believed a falsehood. We must abide daily with Christ so He can purge us of any error that has crept into our thinking.

The Israelites grew up in homes filled with deception. Every time the Israelite children heard their parents grumble against God or Moses, they were exposed to lies. After 40 years of indoctrination, untruths had become firmly lodged in the hearts and minds of these young adults. In this passage, we see three false beliefs that took root in the hearts of the younger generation.

a) A Better Past

Satan often prevents people from experiencing spiritual advance by convincing them that their past was better than their present. Why make sacrifices to move forward if our past is more desirable? Of course, our mind plays tricks on us. It dresses our past up in its finest attire. We soon forget its painful truth while we glamorize its positive aspects. Our past can be extremely seductive once it becomes an idealized fiction.

God is the only one who knows the entire truth of our background. He loves us too much to leave us where we are. Once the apostle Paul saw his previous life as Christ did, he declared he would forget his past and press toward what God had prepared for him (Phil. 3:14). Our past is not necessarily evil, but it is merely a foundation for our future. Those who choose to dwell in the past will forfeit their future.

Believing life was better for the Israelites when they were slaves in Egypt was certainly a stretch of the imagination. Their oppressive taskmasters made their lives miserable. The Israelites had no freedom. Yet the former slaves were deceived into believing their bondage was not as harsh and unpleasant as it actually was. For this reason, spiritual memory is so important. To live wisely today, we must recall both the depths from which God saved us and the heights from which we have fallen (Hos. 11:1-4; Rev. 2:5). Claiming they would be better off dying in the wilderness than advancing into the Promised Land demonstrated how disoriented the people had become to reality. Preferring death to obedience reflects the ultimate spiritual blindness. The great danger of falsehood is that it blinds us to the pathway to life.

b) An Evil Place

A second falsehood the Israelites believed was that the place where God brought them was evil. It is exceedingly unwise to call God's will evil. The place God leads you may be difficult, confusing, and even painful, but it is never evil. Too often God's people mistake difficult for bad. They assume that if life's circumstances are arduous or uncomfortable, God is not their author.

Making hasty evaluations about the place where God leads us is generally unwise. What may appear evil at first glance could become one of the greatest experiences of our life. God does His greatest work under difficult circumstances. The Israelites saw that they had no water to drink and enemies waiting for them on the horizon. Yet God knew He was going to miraculously provide for all of their needs and lead them to spectacular military victories. What appeared to be a hopeless place would become a miraculous place.

Likewise, sometimes we believe our situation is wonderful, but God views it negatively. The Israelites viewed the wilderness as a good place in contrast to Canaan and the dangers therein. But God saw the wilderness for what it was, a sorry substitute for the Promised Land. God refused to call a cheap replica for His will "good." We do not know if our situation is good or evil until we have heard God's evaluation.

By declaring God's will to be "evil," the Israelites were rejecting God's plan and questioning His love. They were evaluating their circumstances based on what they could see, rather than on what God had said. Such an approach inevitably leads to discouragement. If God specifically leads you to Kadesh, it is the best possible place for you to be.

c) Grain, Figs, Pomegranates, and Water

This third complaint is common, especially among those who refuse to trust God. The Israelites bemoaned the fact that Kadesh was barren of grain, figs, pomegranates, and water. At first glance, this concern appears reasonable. After all, everyone needs to eat and drink.

However, two important issues stand out. First, the Israelites had subsisted on a menu of manna for 40 years. While we can sympathize with their desire to diversify their diet, we must also ask why they expected to eat anything else at Kadesh. They had only begun to move toward Canaan. They had not yet entered the Promised Land. Taking preliminary steps toward God's promise does not immediately release all the benefits associated with it. We must not expect a bounteous celebratory feast after only one day's march in the right direction.

There is a second, more troubling issue. The Israelites complained that they had no grain, figs, or pomegranates. Their complaint brings to mind an event that took place 40 years earlier. The twelve spies had just returned from 40 days of reconnoitering Canaan. They found luscious grapes in the land and brought back a cluster so large that two men had to carry it on a pole (Num. 13:23). In addition, the spies declared they found large quantities of pomegranates and figs, and that the land flowed with milk and honey just as God promised (Num. 13:23-27).

Everything the Israelites longed for was waiting for them in abundance in the Promised Land. Nevertheless, the Israelites refused to believe God would keep His word to them. As a result, they chose to dwell fearfully in the wilderness rather than enter Canaan by faith. The reward for faith was a land flowing with milk and honey. The consequence of unbelief was a dreary existence in the desert subsiding on manna. God stopped providing manna only after His people entered the Promised Land (Josh. 5:12). God never intended for the Israelites to eat manna for so long. It was merely a substitute for God's best. However, God refused to bless His people with bounty when they refused to trust Him. Once the Israelites began walking with God by faith, God was pleased to release His riches upon them.

Oh the audacity of the human heart that refuses to obey God's commands, then bitterly complains when He does not bless them. God had placed everything the people desired in the Promised Land. All they had to do was enter it. Yet having refused to occupy Canaan, they bitterly complained that there was no milk or honey in the desert. The Israelites wanted the reward for obedience without obeying! They desired the fruit of faith without believing! God adamantly refused to provide in the wilderness what He promised in the Promised Land. There are no shortcuts to God's promises. There are no substitutes for obedience.

History brims with accounts of those who refused to trust God but demanded that God indulge them with the blessings of obedience. People reject God's standards for marriage, then complain about their miserable home life. Or people refuse to follow God's teaching on financial stewardship, then bemoan the fact they are constantly enduring financial crises. Knowingly disobeying God's clear instruction is one thing. Disobeying and still expecting a reward is quite another.

4.EVALUATING THE SOURCE

One of the most troubling realities of the human experience is that the critic's voice can drown out the voice of almighty God. For every great work of God, there are corresponding critiques, complaints, and doubts. Whenever God launches a new advance, some people are so disoriented to Him that they criticize and complain rather than worship and advance. Cynics and naysayers should never catch leaders off guard. Wherever there are people, there will inevitably be complainers. Such is the reality of the fallen human condition. Some people can only see the negative regardless of how many positive realities swirl about them.

Despite everything leaders know about human nature, such opponents can still catch them off guard. Unwary leaders begin to move forward in obedience to God's instruction. Suddenly, a barrage of criticism assails them. Many godly leaders second-guess themselves. They ask, "If this is God's will, why are so many opposed?" Such leaders may lose their confidence as well as their resolve to move forward.

Wise leaders understand that the fiercest opposition is mobilized at the point of God's greatest advance. Dark forces need not waste time opposing your attendance in bureaucratic committee meetings and mundane religious activity. But find yourself in the center of a great work of God, and a relentless fusillade of venom will bombard you.

Many of God's servants lose heart when opposition arises. Some resign their post claiming their family should not endure such cruel behavior. Others retreat and spend months re-evaluating their approach, worried they might have made a mistake. All the while, the Promised Land beckons on the horizon. Veteran servants of God should not go looking for opposition, but neither should they be surprised when they encounter it. Such is the natural consequence of being light in a darkened world (John 1:5).

CONCLUSION

The Israelites should have been exuberant at finally approaching Kadesh once more. But they were disoriented to God. As a result, God's will confused them. They expected one thing, and God gave them another. They complained when they should have rejoiced. They grumbled when they should have worshipped. Such is the sad irony when God's people do not know His heart and His ways. People may be at the threshold of receiving God's spectacular promises and yet miserably lament their evil circumstances.

QUESTIONS FOR CONSIDERATION

1. Are you at Kadesh right now? If you are, how are you handling it?

2. Are you currently dealing with opposition? If you are, how well are you dealing with it? How do you respond to those who oppose and criticize you?

3. How do you treat your past? Do you view it realistically? How are you using it as a basis for God's work in your life today?

4. How do you view the place God has currently assigned you? Have you been tempted to view it as evil?

5. Have you grown comfortable or complacent in the wilderness? Are you looking for things in a wilderness that God only provides in a Promised Land?

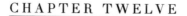

CHAPTER TWELVE

Facing Opposition

"Then Moses and Aaron went from the presence of the assembly to the doorway of the tent of meeting. They fell down with their faces to the ground, and the glory of the Lord appeared to them" (Num. 20:6)

1. THEN

The voices you heed affect your life's direction. When you pay attention to wise counsel, you move in the direction of wisdom. When you listen to faulty or evil opinions, your life proceeds toward destruction. When you indulge in flatterers, you are blinded by pride and in danger of stumbling. When you harken to critics, you can sink to the depths in which they lurk.

Moses was accustomed to criticism. As a young man, the Israelites derided his first attempt to help them (Ex. 2:14). Since that time, his every step had been second-guessed. Moses was unusually humble for a man of his stature (Num. 12:3). Nevertheless, a steady drip of negativity can eventually erode the hardiest soul. We can only imagine how disheartening it was for Moses to hear the same complaints spewing from this new generation of Israelites that he had endured for years from their parents. Moses might have assumed this younger generation would be delighted to finally depart from the wilderness. He might have concluded that 40 years of desert wandering would have immunized them from a complaining spirit. If he had any such hope, it was thoroughly dispelled.

Although we cannot always determine our circumstances, we have absolute control over our response. Though others may act in an ungodly manner toward us, we are entirely free to respond in the spirit of Christ. The word "then" or "so" in this text once again provides a watershed moment. What came next would determine the trajectory of Moses' life.

Many people would have forfeited their leadership at this point. Having grown weary of the constant bickering, they would finally lose their self-control and lash out at their critics. Complainers themselves rarely have the power or influence to seize control of the ship. Rather, they provide a continual irritant to leaders in hopes it will eventually drive them to abdicate their role and leave control to the insurgents. Sadly, what the complainers generally lack in numbers they more than compensate for in venom and volume. When we read "then" in the text, we collectively hold our breath as we wait to see how the beleaguered leader will respond. The critics had spoken. The future hinged on what Moses did next.

2. THE TENT OF MEETING

Moses had to make a choice. He could remain in the presence of his critics and descend into a bitter shouting match. Or, he could remove himself from his challengers and hurriedly make his way into God's presence. Arguing with or debating congenital complainers is supremely unprofitable. In fact, it plays right into their hands, for it grants them an audience and lends them a semblance of legitimacy. Grumblers tend to derive more pleasure in finding fault than they do in finding solutions. They are negative by nature. Regardless of their circumstance, they are determined to be critical. Striving to appease such naysayers is futile, for it is fundamentally impossible. Woe to those leaders who continually attempt to assuage their critics' latest complaints. By so doing, they make the loudest complainer, rather than God, the driving force of their leadership.

Moses and Aaron departed from the presence of the grumblers and hastily made their way to the tent of meeting. They entered the doorway and fell on their faces. This act presents a compelling image. These two men had grown weary from the constant complaining.

They were desperate for God's intervention. They did not go to the center of the tent or to its holiest compartment. Moses and Aaron did not commence a lengthy prayer itemizing their problems. They didn't have to. The key was drawing near to the Lord. God knew the complainers and critics far better than Moses and Aaron did. He heard every accusation. He saw the condition of every heart. Moses understood that if he abided in God's presence, he would receive everything he needed for his current trial.

3.FACES

Moses and Aaron did not merely enter the tent and take a seat in the vestibule. They placed their faces as low to the ground as possible, humbling themselves in dramatic fashion.

Biblically, what we do with our face has significant implications. When the Persian Empire rose to prominence, the monarch was treated as a god. To enter his presence without being summoned, or to stare at the sovereign, was to commit an offense worthy of instant execution. Queen Esther understood that to approach her own husband, the Persian king, without having first been summoned could result in death. It is from the word used to describe people prostrating themselves in abject humiliation before the king that we get the biblical word for "worship." To worship God in this manner involves humbly lowering your face to the lowest point possible. Even the heavenly creatures that wait upon the Lord must cover their faces in His presence. The seraphim that serve before God's throne continually cry, "Holy! Holy! Holy!" Yet they must use one set of wings to cover their faces and another set to cover their feet, for even these magnificent angelic beings tremble in the almighty's presence (Is. 6:2). Those who passed by Jesus while He hung dying on a cross presented an intense contrast to this worshipful behavior. Those rebellious creatures of dust scornfully mocked Him and wagged their heads at him (Matt. 27:39). With our faces we can show either reverence or contempt.

What we do with our face determines what God does with His. When we behave arrogantly or sinfully, God hides His face from us (Is. 59:2). Yet when He is pleased with us, He shines His face upon us (Num. 6:25). Moses desperately needed God to shine His face upon him, so Moses fell on his.

Too many of God's servants make demands on their Lord. They want to negotiate their working conditions and benefits. They claim the right to refrain from serving God if their circumstances are unpleasant. When they meet with God, they vent rather than listen. Though they may feel temporarily better after expressing their anger and frustration to their Master, their situation remains unchanged. Moses and Aaron did not draw near to God in order to complain about the grumblers. They fell on their faces and waited humbly, reverently, and expectantly for a word from their Lord.

4. THE GLORY OF THE LORD

We do not know how long Moses and Aaron remained on their faces. It may have only been a few intense moments, or it may have been all afternoon. We cannot summon God. We can only place ourselves in a posture that invites Him to draw near to us (James 4:8). One thing is clear: Moses did not intend to leave until he heard from God. How often we would experience God's glory if it only required five minutes of urgent entreaty! But God's glory does not fall on a whim or after a superficial, hurried prayer. It descends when we are absolutely desperate. It comes when we have thoroughly humbled ourselves and recognized that all is lost if we do not hear from God. Moses was determined to stay on his face until he received God's answer. Oh that we had the same tenacity!

God is masterful in His dealings with people. He always knows the exact word, the perfect experience, and the most impactful encounters that meet the deepest needs of our life. He handles His servants with such exquisite care that He not only meets their needs, He also transforms their lives. With God, no word is wasted, no experience is redundant, and no encounter is purposeless.

God could have responded to Moses in a multiplicity of ways. He might have dispatched an angel to embolden Moses to stand firm before his critics. God could have coached Moses to know how to refute naysayers. God might have affirmed Moses and strengthened his resolve as a leader. But God did something else.

God granted Moses something far greater than a solution to his problems. God gave Moses Himself. In that sacred tent, God's glory fell. Unless you have experienced this yourself, it is difficult to fully understand what it means. In an instant, the room was filled with the tangible, powerful, holy, awesome presence of God. He removed the veil from Moses and Aaron's eyes so they could experience His overwhelming presence in a personal, intimate way. God's servants often mistakenly believe their primary need is additional funding, more followers, or increased resources. Yet what they require above all else is to experience the glory of the Lord. God would ultimately provide Moses with specific answers to his problem, but God knew Moses had a greater need than logistical solutions to his management problem. When we come to God with questions, His first response is to give us Himself.

In a time of political turmoil, the prophet Isaiah assumed he needed news of a smooth governmental transition. Instead, God offered his troubled prophet a glimpse into heaven's throne room (Is. 6:1-4). Once Isaiah encountered almighty God, we do not hear of him asking for anything more. In a time of military crisis, Elisha's servant was not granted a brigade of elite troops as he might have wished. Instead, God offered him a clear perspective of the divine presence on the battlefield (2 Kings 6:13-17). At times, God's servants can become so consumed with the pressing problems at hand that they neglect to seek a fresh encounter with God. Yet until we are keenly aware of God's presence in the midst of our circumstances, we cannot accurately ascertain the problems we face.

Many of God's servants are ministering year in and year out without a fresh encounter with God. They may have experienced a miraculous conversion years earlier. Perhaps God called them to their current assignment in dramatic fashion. But years have passed and serving God has become routine or even drudgery. Doing God's will has deteriorated into merely carrying out mundane tasks, attending meetings, and administering services and programs. How tragic when a person called by almighty God is reduced to a religious bureaucrat.

Many churches today are well administered. They operate safely within their budget. They meticulously maintain their property. They offer well-planned, choreographed programs and services. But God's glory has departed. In the frenetic pace of Christian service, they hardly miss it. Ministers assume their brimming calendar is evidence of their spirituality. Working hard for God is equated to walking closely with Him. God's servants can grow weary and frustrated in their service, yet trudge on year by year. Sadly, this scenario describes many churches across the land today. They consist of good people doing commendable activities. But God's glory is missing.

Moses knew his situation was desperate. He did not require additional meetings or discussions with people. He desperately needed a word from God. So Moses made his way to the tent of meeting and flung himself inside the doorway. Exhausted, frustrated, and weary, Moses lay on the ground emptied of himself. He did not outline the problem to God as he saw it. He did not lay his requests before his Lord. He simply prostrated himself before God and humbly waited for a fresh word of instruction. And, as Moses expected, God did not disappoint.

CONCLUSION

The key to successful service for God lies not in people's willingness to follow you, but in the intimacy of your walk with God. Inevitably you will encounter a problem or circumstance that is beyond you. Don't be discouraged. God may use your circumstances to draw you back to Himself. Your walk with God will empower you to effectively minister to others. Jesus declared that apart from our abiding relationship with Him, we could do nothing (John 15:5). If you have recently encountered that truth, hurry back to the tent of meeting, fall on your face, and wait as long as necessary until the glory falls.

QUESTIONS TO CONSIDER

1. Have you been listening more to people's voices or God's? How has that been affecting you?

2. Do you need to have a fresh encounter with the Lord? If so, what lengths are you willing to go until

you do? Is God still waiting for you to properly humble yourself?

3. Where is your tent of meeting? Where do you go to meet with your Lord?

4. When you meet with God, how much do you speak and how much do you listen? How long are you willing to wait until you hear from God?

5. In all your praying and worship, when was the last time you experienced the tangible presence and glory of the Lord? Do you long for a deeper encounter with God than you have ever experienced before?

CHAPTER THIRTEEN

God's Answer

"The Lord spoke to Moses, 'Take the staff and assemble the community. You and your brother Aaron are to speak to the rock while they watch, and it will yield its water. You will bring out water for them from the rock and provide drink for the community and their livestock" (Num. 20:7-8).

1. THE LORD SPOKE

You are always one divine word away from a radically altered condition. With a word, God brought the universe into existence, raised the dead to life, calmed a storm, and routed a legion of demons. When you face difficult circumstances, you may want to talk to your staff, banker, or friends. But one word from God is infinitely superior to ten thousand words uttered by others.

Scripture tells us that God spoke to Moses. We are not informed if God spoke with an audible voice or if He communicated directly to Moses' mind. Throughout Scripture, God spoke to people in numerous ways. Occasionally God sent angels to deliver a message. At other times God communicated through a dream, vision, or prophet. Sometimes God spoke audibly. The key was never *how* God spoke, but *that* He spoke. Scripture clearly reveals a God who interacts with His servants as He accomplishes His purposes through them.

Too many people serve God without communing with Him. They do what makes sense to them. They draw upon previous experience. They seek advice from friends and advisors. They make lists of pros and cons. But they do not seek a word from God. Moses had no answer for the problem he faced. Neither did his friends or colleagues. No amount of brainstorming with his top associates would have led Moses to conclude that the answer to his dilemma lay in speaking to a rock! Without a word from God, disaster was imminent.

2. THE ROD

When God spoke, He did not merely give Moses a principle. God revealed a specific course of action. He instructed Moses to take the rod with him. When God first called Moses to deliver the Israelites from Egypt, Moses argued that he was incapable of the immense task.

In response, God asked, *"What is that in your hand?"* (Ex. 4:2). Moses was grasping his rod. He had used it throughout the years as a shepherd. God told him to cast it to the ground. It immediately became a serpent. God did not put something new into Moses' hand, He simply took what Moses already possessed and transformed it into something greater.

God instructed Moses to take his shepherd's tool with him to Egypt. God intended to use what Moses had surrendered to him in order to accomplish His purposes (Ex. 4:17). Moses held his rod over the Nile River and the water turned to blood (Ex. 7:15). He lifted his rod and a violent hailstorm ensued (Ex. 9:23). He raised his rod and a plague of locusts descended upon the land (Ex. 10:13). Moses' rod not only represented his call into service, it also symbolized the many times God had empowered Moses to accomplish seemingly impossible tasks. Now, facing yet another challenge, God instructed His servant to take that rod with him once more. The rod did not possess magical qualities. Moses' power came from God. So why did God tell Moses to take the rod with him? Perhaps God was reminding Moses of his calling. When God's servants face opposition and crises, God's call on their life is often what sustains them. Perhaps the rod was a reminder that God had never failed Moses before. Whatever means God intended to use to aid His beleaguered servant this time, He would utilize the same power and effectiveness with which He had assisted Moses in times past.

3.SPEAK TO THE ROCK

Moses may have anticipated God's further instructions. After all, Moses and the Israelites had faced this dilemma before. A generation earlier, the Israelites had camped at Rephidim (Ex. 17:1-7). There they faced desert dwellers' constant predicament: no water. The people complained and God answered. In that instance, God told Moses to gather the people before the rock. He was to strike the rock and water would pour forth. Moses did exactly as God instructed and he experienced miraculous success.

Decades later, Moses might have expected God to give him identical instructions. After all, how many methods does someone require to bring water out of a rock? If a technique worked in the past, certainly it should be sufficient in the future. At first, the instructions are identical. God instructs Moses to gather the leaders before the rock. This detail placed a certain onus on Moses. God did not allow Moses to lead from a safe distance in his ministerial office. Moses invited his most virulent opponents to witness God's power first hand.

God also instructed Moses to take the rod with him. This instruction seems curious. In Exodus 17, we understand why God told Moses to do this, for he needed to strike the rock with it. But this time God told Moses simply to speak to the rock. This instruction raises two questions.

First, why did God adjust His methodology? Moses had already brought water from a rock by striking it. Surely God wanted Moses to be successful. Why then did

God complicate matters by asking him to speak to the rock when Moses had already demonstrated a proficiency at striking rocks?

God did not explain His reasoning, so we can only speculate. But one thing is certain: bringing forth water by speaking to a rock is a markedly greater miracle than striking a rock to produce water. We might imagine that after Moses struck the rock at Rephidim, skeptics gathered around the rock to discover Moses' tricks. They may have suspected that Moses knew where a spring was located and that he had placed a rock over its surface. Perhaps in striking the rock, Moses had dislodged a plug so water could come forth. We can imagine the doubters trying to dismiss the miracle. But how could they explain water springing forth at the sound of Moses' voice? Clearly that was a greater miracle than Moses performed the first time.

Why would God care if Moses accomplished a greater miracle than he had previously? Because the greater the miracle, the greater the glory Moses brought to God. Our primary purpose on earth is to glorify our Creator (Rom. 11:36). God seeks to elevate the level of our divine service to new heights. Doing what he had successfully accomplished before would not require any great faith from Moses. So God adjusted the plan. God was not allowing Moses to rest in the spiritual success of the past. God was determined to do a fresh work through His servant's life.

Too often God's servants use a faulty definition of the word "faithful" to describe their work. These veteran ministers do the same thing, the same way, garnering the same results, year after year. Because they have remained at their post for an extended period they assume they have been faithful. But in God's eyes, those who are faithful are those who are growing and bearing much fruit (Matt. 25:21). God delights in doing a greater work through His servant than He has done previously. He refuses to leave people where they have always been. Even a spiritual giant such as Moses would learn that when you serve the Lord, there are always greater heights to which He can raise your service. Truly faithful servants are eager to ascend there.

That being said, we come back to the confusing instruction. God told Moses to take his staff with him. Why? As we have seen, the staff reminded Moses of his calling and God's provision. Nevertheless, Moses would not require a staff simply to speak to the rock. The staff itself had no magical powers. God wasn't implying that it was Moses' magical wand or good luck charm. So why did God command Moses to take it with him? Would its presence not confuse the issue?

Perhaps a related question is this: Why did God place the tree of the knowledge of good and evil in the Garden of Eden if He had forbidden Adam and Eve from eating its fruit? It is because God values free will. He was giving Moses a choice. Moses could trust God to do a greater work through his life than he had done before, or he could resort to methods that had been successful in the past. One of the most seductive temptations leaders face is previous accomplishment. Leaders are not lured by yesterday's failures. But yesterday's triumphs are supremely difficult to release from their grasp.

Moses was going to stand before an entire crowd of doubters and complainers and attempt something new. What if he failed? What if he appeared foolish? Might it not be more prudent to use a tried and true method? Clutching the rod in his hand, Moses had to decide if he would step out in faith and trust God with something new, or if he would default to a process that had worked previously.

One of our greatest struggles is deciding if we will place our faith in a Person or in a method. An idol is anything that takes God's place in our life. If we turn to it for provision when God instructed us to turn to Him for that answer, it is an idol. The Ark of the Covenant eventually became an idol to the Israelites, so God removed it (1 Sam. 4:3-11). Later, God's people placed their faith in the temple building rather than in the temple Occupant, so God allowed it to be obliterated.

Successful methods are incredibly enticing. Desperately craving achievement, people willingly forfeit their relationship with God so long as they achieve their goals. Perhaps this reality is why God rarely does the same thing twice. He does not want His people to idolize a method. God only told the Israelites to march around a walled city seven times on one occasion. As spectacularly successful as that method was, the key was not marching around a city. The key was doing what God said. Only once did God instruct a general to whittle his army down to 300 soldiers and then to blow trumpets and hold up torches in the middle of the night. This method was so resoundingly effective one would think God would have repeatedly utilized it. But He did not. Since He has a limitless number of methods at His disposal, God prefers to change His approach, requiring us to continually depend on Him. God asked Moses to do a supremely difficult thing: to walk away from success and trust God for something new. After having journeyed with God for so long and seeing Him perform so many spectacular miracles, had Moses learned that his success lay not in the means God used, but in the God who gave him the means?

4. SO

"So Moses took the staff from the Lord's presence just as He had commanded him" (Num. 20:9).

"So" is a seemingly inconsequential word. It simply links what happened previously with what is about to transpire. Based on what God said, Moses will act. Some Christian "pragmatists" love to criticize those who seek to abide in Christ. These individuals view themselves as people of action. They grow restless if they remain still in God's presence for any length of time. They prefer to be "proactive" rather than "reactive." They believe any action is better than waiting. To them, those who seek a word from God are shunning their responsibility for action. But what these people misunderstand is that, after you receive a word from God, there will inevitably be a "so" that is forthcoming. An encounter with God always leads to a response. Abiding in Christ does not lead to inaction, but to God-sized activity. Moses did not immediately respond to the people's complaints. Rather, he took time to seek a word from God. Once he met with God, Moses was prepared not only to solve a problem, but to be at the center of a miracle.

As we have seen, God's servants face a series of "so's" throughout the course of their life and ministry. These watershed moments occur when they clearly know God's will. Then the word "so" presents itself. Based on what God said, what will His servant do? God's word is unchanging. Our response to His word varies greatly!

At this point in the story we are hopeful. Moses had indeed faced a difficult challenge, but he handled it with grace and humility. He sought a word from the Lord and he received one.

A word from God is an awesome responsibility. For, to whom much has been given, much is required (Luke 12:48). Once God utters a divine word, it is a sacred trust. One should never be careless or lackadaisical about handling a heavenly directive. The sooner we obey and implement God's command the better. Moses immediately departed from the tent of meeting and took action.

However, the distance between hearing God's word and obeying it can sometimes seem like a marathon, with mine fields ominously laid along the path. Many well-intentioned Christians have commenced their journey of obedience only to meet catastrophe and ruin along the way. There is an enormous chasm between good intentions and obedience. Obedience is often difficult. Opposition will attempt to thwart our divine service. Our determination can waver. Our resolve can weaken. Our focus can be distracted. Though a multitude may boldly march toward the goal of divine obedience, only a remnant typically arrives at the destination. Sadly, Moses will become one of the casualties. He begins well, but he will end in catastrophe.

CONCLUSION

Despite bearing the responsibility for an entire nation, Moses never shortened or cancelled his personal time with God. It was there that he found answers unavailable to him elsewhere. Moses' relationship with God was dynamic, not static. God gave him fresh, unique messages at just the right time. Moses never left his time alone with God without greater insight, confidence, and resolve to accomplish God's will. Remaining discouraged is exceedingly difficult when you regularly meet with, hear from, and are deeply impacted by the living God. Do you need to hurriedly withdraw into God's sacred presence and hear afresh what He has on his heart for you?

QUESTIONS TO CONSIDER

1. Are you comfortable seeking specific direction from God, or do you prefer to solve your own problems?

2. How have you been tempted to trust in a method rather than in God? What has made the method so attractive to you?

3. Are you facing a divine "so" in your life right now? How long has it been since you knew what God wanted you to do?

4. Has God been positioning your life so you experienced a greater miracle than you have before? If He has, how have you trusted Him in that process?

5. Are you still using outdated methods that once brought you success but now have grown stale?

CHAPTER FOURTEEN

Rebels

1. IN FRONT OF THE ROCK

"Moses and Aaron summoned the assembly in front of the rock . . . " (Num. 20:10).

O pposition and criticism have a sinister way of penetrating our normally reliable defenses and unsettling our heart in ways other trials do not. Moses was typically a humble man (Num. 12:3). He had just experienced a profound encounter with God in which he received fresh instructions from his Lord. In light of what God had just done in Moses' life, we don't anticipate the angry, prideful invective that will soon erupt.

Moses' problem was not that his critics pressured him into bitter, God-dishonoring speech. Rather, his opponents dislodged pride and anger from the hidden

187

depths of his soul, allowing them to emerge into the bright light of public perception. Throughout his years of admirable service, Moses had never fully surrendered the last bastions of anger and pride in his heart. Despite all he had experienced of God's holiness and power, Moses still clung to some of the worst aspects of his character. There is a profound difference between suppressing an ugly character trait and transforming it. At a vulnerable moment, under certain conditions, Moses' pride waited to emerge from hiding to inflict mortal damage.

God's servants must be wary of sinful impulses lingering below the surface of their character. Just because such traits remain in hiding does not mean they no longer pose a threat. They may have simply withdrawn behind the walls of their stronghold, waiting for an opportune time to take up arms and strike a blow against God's supremacy. David pleaded, *"Search me, God, and know my heart; test me and know my concerns. See if there is any offensive way in me . . ."* (Ps. 139:23-24). He knew full well the lethal nature of hidden sin. After experiencing repeated success as God's anointed, David suffered a near-fatal ambush in a careless moment when his sinful urges emerged from hiding and attempted to bring him to ruin. The great warrior experienced repeated success over his enemies until he became careless of the fact that his greatest enemy was entrenched in the strongholds of his own heart.

Wise Christians accept the grim truth that there can be no truce with sin. Our sympathy must never lie with it. Regardless of our difficult past, our painful trials, or our heavy burden, we dare not sympathize with or tolerate anything that God declares to be evil. Our sin hates us and has but one goal: to destroy us. A cessation of hostilities is insufficient. We can achieve no lasting peace or freedom until every remnant of unrighteousness in our life has been ruthlessly identified, defeated, and put to death.

Moses and Aaron summoned the assembly before the rock as God commanded. Again, this seemingly innocuous detail will have profound implications. Thus far, Moses had explicitly followed God's commands. However, acts of obedience have multiple implications. Moses assembled an audience, which raised the stakes for his obedience. Leaders function on a public stage. It is the nature of their calling. Leaders are granted broader visibility that enables them to exert greater influence for good or ill than the average person. Every time leaders stand before an audience, they assume a greater degree of accountability. That truth is why the apostle James cautioned people about assuming the role of teacher, for they will receive a stricter judgment (James 3:1). When we sin in secret, we invite God to deal with us privately, though He reserves the right to shout our transgression from the rooftops (Luke 12:3). But when we sin publicly, we will most certainly be judged before others. As a result, by summoning the nation's leaders, Moses put his obedience to God on public display. Every pair of eyes watching Moses heightened the level of accountability and judgment he would face for his actions. Leadership is conducted "before the rock." People watch and emulate their leaders. This fundamental reality of leadership would ultimately cost Moses dearly.

2. REBELS

> *". . . and Moses said to them, 'Listen, you rebels! Must we bring water out of this rock for you?'"* (Num. 20:10).

Until this moment, Moses' behavior had been exemplary. He refused to descend into acrimony when his opponents criticized him. Instead, he hurried into God's presence. Moses did not argue or make excuses when God told him how to respond to the people's need. Rather, he humbly received his marching orders. When Moses' meeting with God ended, he did not linger or delay, but immediately began implementing God's directives. Thus far we have every reason to assume Moses was on his way to another successful act of service.

Then something went terribly wrong. Moses' statement catches us by surprise. What is particularly disturbing is that what spewed from Moses' mouth revealed what was in his heart (Matt. 15:18). We are stunned to discover that after all these years pride had maintained a stronghold in Moses' life.

"Hear now you rebels." This statement is profoundly ironic. Moses pronounced judgment on those who stood before him. He had heard enough to determine they

were rebels. But, as typically occurs with people who have become disoriented to God, Moses had become a hypocrite.

Moses went off script. He certainly believed his words were true. Perhaps he hoped such a scathing denunciation might shame the people into repentance. But God did not give him this message. It may have been factual, but it was not faithful. Preachers and Bible teachers have long served with the acute awareness that adding to what God says is as heretical and dangerous as subtracting from God's words. God's spokespersons are obligated to deliver the message as carefully and accurately as possible. The people may have assumed Moses would return from the tent of meeting with a message from God. But Moses had amalgamated God's word with his own perspective, which is always a hazardous undertaking.

Moses presumed to sit in judgment over those to whom he ministered (Matt. 7:1). Such behavior is precarious and normally undergirded by pride. The people had complained and expressed discontent, yet God did not condemn them for their behavior. In fact, God responded by providing an answer to their problems. Moses took it upon himself to make a ruling on the people's hearts and walk with God.

Leaders do well to love, lead, and serve their people, but they enter uncertain waters when they pronounce judgment on them. We do not know what lies in people's hearts. We cannot discern their motives. We can observe the fruitfulness of people's lives, but we always run the risk of being too harsh or condemning. We are certainly on thin ice when we place ourselves in a judgment seat that belongs exclusively to God.

Moses' action was particularly ironic because, even as he pointed an accusing finger at the crowd, he was the most brazen rebel on the premises. None of those complaining Hebrews were banned from the Promised Land because of their behavior that day. But Moses was. The person God dealt with most harshly was the one condemning everyone else!

The sins that disturb us most in others are often the very ones we struggle with ourselves. Why do we react so strongly to those who desire control? Perhaps we covet power ourselves. Why are we so repelled by others' pride? Perhaps because their hubris offends our ego. Just as a doctor looks for soreness in our flesh in order to detect infection beneath the skin, when we react strongly to the sins in others, God may be alerting us to evil dwelling within us. Of all the accusations Moses might have leveled against the Israelites, he chose the offense of rebellion. This decision should not surprise us, for it was rebellion that broke forth in Moses' own heart. What behaviors, attitudes, and words of others disturb you most? What might that reveal about you?

3. WE

While supplementing a divine message is a dangerous presumption, taking credit for God's activity is even more dangerous. This simple two-letter English word is

Moses' undoing. Moses crossed a line at this point from which he could not return. It would forever cloud his future.

Who brought water from the rock at Rephidim (Ex. 17:1-7)? God. No one believed Moses was responsible. Who unleashed plagues upon Egypt, parted the Red Sea, and provided manna? God had done it all. Moses served God for so long that he began to identify his efforts with God's work. He dared to touch God's glory. God declared: *"I am Yahweh, that is My name; I will not give My glory to another . . ."* (Is. 42:8). God is a jealous God. He is intensely possessive of His people's worship (Ex. 34:14). He is supremely jealous of His glory. He will not share it.

Moses committed an unpardonable sin. In brazenly elevating himself before others, he inadvertently lowered God in people's eyes. Throughout the course of Moses' life, he had been inexorably drawn to the brilliant light of God's glory. Years earlier Moses merely wanted to observe God's glory (Ex. 33:18). In those sacred moments, almighty God shielded Moses in the cleft of a rock so he would not be consumed by God's awesome holiness. As Moses communed with God in subsequent meetings, his face glowed from the reflected glory of God's majesty (Ex. 34:29-35). Yet in a candid moment of anger, Moses revealed the location of evil's stronghold in his heart. In fact, Moses had the effrontery to take credit before God even acted! In stark contrast, when Jesus performed a miracle before a crowd, people came away thinking more highly of His Father (Luke 9:43).

In his supreme insolence, Moses diminished God and magnified himself. To make matters worse, Moses did so publicly. All of heaven may have gasped. Perhaps not since Lucifer sought to usurp God's glory had one of God's prominent servants acted so arrogantly. We know God is longsuffering and gracious, but He responds quickly and resoundingly to certain public sins. Before this account is over, this audacious act of rebellion will be decisively dealt with.

4. STRIKING THE ROCK

> *"Then Moses raised his hand and struck the rock twice with his staff . . ."* (Num. 20:11).

Moses spoke incorrectly about God. Then he dared to stretch out his hand to touch the divine glory. One sin inevitably leads to another. Next he raised his hand and struck the rock, twice. He decided to trust a method rather than God. Raising his hand implies he hit the rock with force. God told him to speak to the rock. Doing so required little effort but much faith. Striking the rock required much effort and little faith. How hard do you have to strike a rock in the desert before water spews forth from it? When you attempt to do God's work in your own strength, you cannot strike the rock hard or often enough.

This truth may explain the epidemic rate in which Christian ministers are burning out. Speaking to a rock will never exhaust you. But striking a rock with all your might eventually will. God's assignments will never debilitate a minister, for with each task, God grants the necessary strength. But when we undertake God's work in our own power, we inevitably grow weary. Why did Moses strike the rock twice? He may have been uncertain if one strike would be sufficient. Perhaps he struck the rock at Rephidim twice (Ex. 17:1-7). We are under the impression that, with all his critics gathered before him, Moses was determined to strike the rock as many times as necessary until a stream of water broke forth. Sadly, pride reduced this great man of God to angrily pummeling a rock with his staff in hopes that water would eventually spew forth and assuage his pride before his skeptical audience.

CONCLUSION

When we seek to exalt God's name, all of heaven rallies to aid our endeavor. However, even the greatest ministers can be seduced into taking for themselves what belongs exclusively to God. Though we disguise our hubris with all manner of pious camouflage, God sees our heart clearly. The moment our efforts become self-focused rather than God-centered, the divine equipping and anointing is withdrawn. How tragic to see the religious field littered with prideful ministers feverishly pounding upon dry rocks, wondering where the power and glory of God has gone.

QUESTIONS TO CONSIDER

1. Are you keenly aware of the rock before which you are serving your Lord? Who will be directly affected, negatively or positively, by your example?

2. Are there areas of your character that cause you problems as you serve the Lord? Are there strongholds in your life you have never fully surrendered to Christ? What might you do to finally, and wholly, yield them to Christ?

3. Have you been wearying yourself striking at a rock that God told you to speak to?

4. What annoys you most about others? What does that reveal about what is in your own heart?

5. Have you dared to sit in the judgment seat of Christ?

6. Are you meticulously delivering the messages God has given you, or have you presumed to amend it to your own bias and viewpoint?

CHAPTER FIFTEEN

Hallowed

". . . a great amount of water gushed out, and the community and their livestock drank." (Num. 20:11).

1. WATER

This passage is filled with peculiarities. God explicitly instructed Moses to speak to the rock to procure water. Moses disobeyed God's word, dishonoring Him so arrogantly he would consequently be banished from the Promised Land. Yet right on cue, water spewed from the rock. Why would God seemingly honor Moses' disobedience? Parents instinctively recognize that if they give their children instructions, they dare not reward them if they disobey. Doing so would demonstrate poor parenting.

Moses clearly ignored God's command, but God sent water right on schedule. Leaders must humbly bow their heads here. For if God chose to punish people every time their leader fell short of God's standard, they would suffer extremely bleak and dreary lives. The truth is that God blesses His people primarily in one of two ways. First, God blesses His people *through* their leader. This method is certainly God's preference. Second, God may choose to bless His people *despite* their leader. Sadly, God must use this method when leaders are disoriented to Him.

The people's need for water was not excessive. Without it, they would soon perish. Their lack of faith and complaining was disappointing, but their request was reasonable. God ultimately provided water because they required it to live. However, God was robbed of the glory He might have received had Moses obeyed Him fully.

At times, a minister of a growing church will be exposed for having lived immorally. Occasionally people will exclaim, "If what our pastor did was so wrong, why did God bless the church?" Yet we must never mistake God's provision for His blessing. God loves His people. He longs to provide for them and to bless them. God desires to equip churches to dispel the darkness from their neighborhoods and to make disciples of all nations. But providing for His people's needs does not necessarily indicate God is pleased with their leader. God may bless the church despite its leaders rather than because of them.

2. SHOWING GOD'S HOLINESS

"But the Lord said to Moses and Aaron, 'Because you did not trust Me to show My holiness in the sight of the Israelites, you will not bring this assembly into the land I have given them. These are the waters of Meribah, where the Israelites quarreled with the Lord . . . " (Num. 20:12-13).

This passage is among the most shocking in the Old Testament. Moses is the towering luminary of its pages. He is a nation builder, miracle worker, prophet, songwriter, lawgiver, and general. Notice how Scripture sums up his life: *"No prophet has arisen again in Israel like Moses, whom the Lord knew face to face. He was unparalleled for all the signs and wonders the Lord sent him to do against the land of Egypt—to Pharaoh, to all his officials and to all his land, and for the terrifying deeds that Moses performed in the sight of all Israel"* (Deut. 34:10-11). No one other than the Son of God had such an impressive resume! No other Israelite had fearlessly wrought such miracles before the most powerful monarch of his day. No one else had parted a sea. No one else had led the nation for 40 years while providing the vast multitude with food and water in the desert. No one else had talked face-to-face with God or received the law from God's own hand. Moses' life was unparalleled.

Yet though Moses might have been the greatest of men, he was but a lowly servant before God. And he, like every other person, was accountable for his actions. God informed Moses that he and Aaron would not enter the Promised Land because they failed to hallow God that day.

Our sympathy naturally turns to Moses. We all make mistakes. We have all fallen short. After all Moses had done for the Israelites' cause, surely an accommodation could be made for his momentary indiscretion. Yet God allowed no room for appeal. Moses had dishonored God publicly, and God would punish him in full view of the nation.

God had clearly told Moses what to do. Yet Moses had not only adjusted God's commands to suit his preferences, he had taken God's glory for himself. Worse yet, he had done so before the entire nation. All eyes were on Moses as the people waited to see how God would treat His premier servant. Gasps must have erupted throughout the camp when the Israelites learned that Moses would no longer accompany them into the Promised Land.

We must be careful where we place our sympathies. We naturally feel sorry for Moses, for we see a man who waited 120 years to fulfill his dreams learn that they will never come to pass. We witness a tragically flawed man who meant well, but whose stubbornly rebellious people occasionally pushed him past his limits. We might be tempted to believe God was too harsh on His most outstanding and reliable servant.

But our sympathies must lie with God. He had been working out His purposes for the Israelites long before Moses arrived on the scene. He had spent 40 years with His people in the wilderness teaching them that His words were their life (Deut. 30:11-20). God issues commands, not suggestions. Yet His people continually doubted and rejected His word. Then Moses, who of all people should have known better, amended God's clear directive to be more to his liking. Almighty God could not allow Moses' rebellion to go unpunished. An entire nation learned that day that absolutely no one is exempt from obedience to God's commands. They also witnessed the devastating truth that one sin can negate years of obedience. Oh that we hated sin as much as God does!

3.HALLOWED

"These are the waters of Meribah, where the Israelites quarreled with the Lord, and He showed His holiness to them" (Num. 20:13).

Thus we reach the tragic conclusion of our narrative. It began with such promise as the Israelites broke camp and Moses finally prepared to lead the people into the Promised Land. But a mere 13 verses later, Moses' life dream was shattered and he was consigned to live out the remainder of his days under the shadow of his disobedience. Though Moses would later beg God to rescind His verdict, God remained resolute (Deut. 3:23-27). Moses failed to treat God as holy before the people. For that he paid a terrible price.

Scripture concludes this account with an intriguing statement: *"and He showed His holiness to them"* (Num. 20:13). This phrase is puzzling because the reason Moses could not enter Canaan was, *"Because you did not trust Me to show My holiness in the sight of the Israelites . . ."* (Num. 20:12). Moses did not have the faith required to honor God. As a result, Moses dishonored God when he could have brought Him great glory.

Without faith, it is impossible to please God (Heb. 11:6). Therefore, God will inevitably ask us to do things that appear impossible to us (Is. 55:8-9). In response, we will be tempted to modify God's commands, transforming them into what we believe is reasonable, affordable, and possible. Moses had not trusted God, and therefore he failed to hallow God.

This event's conclusion is surprising: *"and He showed His holiness to them"* (Num. 20:13). Had Moses obeyed God, God would have been glorified through his faithfulness. However, since Moses failed to hallow God, how was God ultimately exalted? God glorified Himself by disciplining His servant. When God humbles a leader, onlookers ultimately think less of the leader and more of God.

God glorified Himself in a similar way when he humbled the prideful King Uzziah. After the monarch achieved great success, his heart filled with pride, and he acted presumptuously before God (2 Chron. 26:16-21). As a result, God struck the mighty king with leprosy, forcing him to live in humiliating isolation for the remainder of his life. Can you imagine what the people of Judah thought when they passed King Uzziah's humble abode? The once mighty king's leprosy now precluded him from occupying the royal palace. Uzziah presumed he could worship God on his own terms. As a result, he was forbidden from ever entering the temple again. Though God forgave Uzziah his sin, the chastened king lived with the consequences of his insolence for the remainder of his days. Uzziah was one of the greatest rulers in Judah's history, yet when he dared to touch God's glory, God thoroughly humbled him.

God dealt with Moses in a manner that caused every Israelite to tremble. If even the mighty Moses could not disregard God's word with impunity, how much more so were the common people obliged to heed God's every word? God can use our life to encourage others, or He can use our example to provide a dire warning.

Moses didn't finish well. Though he experienced spectacular victories as he served God, he also experienced some humiliating failures. Ultimately it is not how we begin to serve God that matters as much as how our service draws to a close. The apostle Paul was able to triumphantly proclaim: *"I have fought the good fight, I have finished the race, I have kept the faith"* (2 Tim. 4:7). Tragically, Moses stumbled at the finish line.

CONCLUSION

History's pages are filled with stories of mighty kings and gallant generals who paraded across the world stage with invincible armies at their back. Yet one by one, these larger-than-life figures succumbed to their mortality and were swept from the pages of history. Yet One remains. Almighty God, the author of history, the vanquisher of insurgents, the judge of humanity, resolutely marches on while accomplishing His every purpose. As this account draws to a close, Moses, the greatest leader of his day, humbly approaches his end, while almighty God prepares His next servant, Joshua, to carry out His further wishes. Human history has unfolded this way throughout the centuries. History is not a chronicle of great people. It is the account of a great God who accomplishes His purposes through frail, unreliable, mortal men and women. In every generation, God looks for those prepared to serve Him with all of their hearts, to cling to His word, and to honor Him in word and in deed.

QUESTIONS FOR CONSIDERATION

1. Is God blessing your family, church, and friends because of you or despite you?

2. Is your life bringing glory to God? If it is, is it because of your obedience or by the way God is disciplining your disobedience?

3. When people observe your life, do they think more highly of God or more highly of you?

4. What area of your life is currently robbing God of the glory due Him?

5. What adjustments do you need to make so your life is as honoring to God as it should be?

6. Are you finishing well? What will you be remembered for? What will your legacy be?

CONCLUSION

The great saints of Scripture and history tower before us. As we study their lives, we wonder what it must feel like to know God so intimately, to exercise God's power so authoritatively, and to exert influence over nations so resoundingly. "Ordinary" people like us soon dismiss biblical examples such as Abraham, Moses, Joshua, Deborah, Elijah, Mary, Peter, and Paul as belonging to an entirely different spiritual class than us. We assume their faith must have been immune to doubt, their courage unmoved by opposition, and their prayers always grand and confident.

But the truth is that every spiritual giant throughout history had feet of clay. They were, without exception, flawed people. What distinguished them was not their intelligence, eloquence, or organizational genius, but their walk with God. Each sought God until they knew Him, loved Him, heard Him, trusted Him, and obeyed Him. Others may have been more qualified, but these biblical giants became more sanctified.

Elijah and Moses are classic examples, not of what talented people can do for God, but what almighty God can accomplish through any person wholly surrendered to Him. As we have seen, Moses and Elijah had many similarities. Both experienced rejection. Both faced bitter opposition. Both spent time in a wilderness. Both grew discouraged. Both prematurely assumed their service for God was over.

But they also shared positive qualities. Both met with God atop Mount Sinai. Both wrought unprecedented miracles. Both boldly pronounced God's word to ungodly rulers. Both spoke with God. Both saw miraculous answers to their prayers. Both prepared a successor. And finally, they were both summoned to personally encourage Jesus on the Mount of Transfiguration.

Moses and Elijah are a study in contrasts. At one moment they boldly pronounced God's message before a pagan, hostile court. Yet at other times they ran for their lives, bitterly resigning their post. On some occasions they spoke with resounding confidence. Later they were wracked with fear and doubt. If we cannot identify with their greatest triumphs, most of us easily resonate with their abject failures. Were we simply to chronicle their shortcomings, we could naturally conclude that they were unfit to be God's servants. They simply had too many problems, doubts, and fears. Yet, when we look at what God accomplished through these frail people, we are astounded to realize that God achieved some of His most spectacular accomplishments through His most ordinary servants.

The one constant in these men's lives was God. He continually worked out His purposes in their lives, even when they lost heart. These men faced extremely difficult challenges, yet God skillfully guided them. The most powerful, evil leaders of their age hated them, yet

God was their shield. Moses and Elijah would at times stand alone, yet those solitary moments led to some of their greatest encounters with God.

Jesus said: *"I am the vine, you are the branches. The one who remains in Me and I in him produces much fruit, because you can do nothing without Me"* (John 15:5). Abiding in Christ is the secret to success with God. It is not our natural inclination. We tend to be self-centered, focusing on our own strengths, weaknesses, fears, and sense of entitlement. We obsess over how people treat us. Pride erects strongholds in our heart. Yet the more we focus on ourselves, the more distant God's voice sounds.

Jesus understood that a disciple who was self-centered or people-focused could accomplish nothing for His kingdom. But those who yielded themselves fully to their Lord would experience the profound truth that, with God, all things are possible.

So it is in our day. Our world has its own Pharaohs, Ahabs, and Jezebels who cause heartache and promote evil with feverish intensity. We can easily give such people our attention. Life also invariably leads us into wilderness seasons. At such times, fixating on the parched, seemingly lifeless desert is easier than focusing on the God who wishes to meet with us in the wasteland.

Elijah and Moses teach us that God is just as present on the mountaintop as He is in the wilderness. God loves us just as much when the crowds shout our praises as when our enemies plot our downfall. God's power is just as mighty when He sends fire from heaven as when He tells us to flee for our lives.

Elijah and Moses also demonstrated that our relationship with God changes over time. It isn't meant to remain static. Sometimes He may speak to us with fire. At other times He may whisper. When facing one problem God may ask us to strike a rock. On a different occasion He might ask us to speak to the stone. God changes methods, even good ones, so we learn to find our joy and strength from our relationship with Him, not from circumstances or a method.

Elijah and Moses learned that the key to their success and joy lay not in achieving their goals, being appreciated by those they served, or peace and prosperity, but solely in their relationship with God. Both men ultimately came to understand that, as long as God was with them, they had more than enough. True joy flowed from their communion with the almighty.

Oh that God's servants would learn these lessons well! Enemies abound, yet God has never been more available to us. Evil is at work, but God is steadfastly carrying out His eternal purposes. People may forsake us, but God remains scrupulously faithful. Others may harm us, but in God's presence is fullness of joy (Ps. 16:11).

No doubt you have experienced failure, rejection, or opposition. You may currently reside in a spiritual wilderness. Life may seem exceedingly harsh and unfair. Yet you cannot determine the reality of your situation until you spend time abiding in Christ. Proper perspective is only possible in His presence. After you hear from God, truth becomes evident. Apart from your abiding relationship with Christ, you cannot bear spiritual fruit (John 15:5). If you depart from your intimate walk with God, you cannot finish well.

May I encourage you to carefully consider the examples of Elijah and Moses? Your relationship with Christ is the most important factor in your life and ministry. If you have become distracted with much service, quickly make you way back into Christ's presence (Luke 10:40). Turn your attention from your enemy's threats and listen intently to your Savior's loving voice. All is not lost! Christ still sits upon His throne! Draw near to Him and He will draw near to you (James 4:8). Let Him love you, heal you, restore you, and strengthen you and, in His good time, He will also commission you. You may be in a wilderness at the moment, but be of good courage, another mountaintop awaits!

ABOUT THE AUTHOR

 **Dr. Richard Blackaby** has been a pastor, a seminary president, and is currently the president of Blackaby Ministries International. He has coauthored numerous books with his father, Henry, including: *Experiencing God: Revised Edition, Spiritual Leadership: Moving People on to God's Agenda, Fresh Encounter, Hearing God's Voice, Experiencing God: Day by Day, Called to Be God's Leader: Lessons from the Life of Joshua, Being Still With God, God in the Marketplace and Flickering Lamps: Christ and His Church.* He also authored: *Putting a Face on Grace: Living a Life Worth Passing On, Unlimiting God, The Seasons of God, Experiencing God at Home, The Inspired Leader,* and *Rebellious Parenting: Daring to Break the Rules So Your Child Can Thrive.* Richard works with Christian CEOs of corporate America and speaks internationally on various topics including spiritual leadership in the church, the home, and the marketplace.

You can follow him at:

Twitter: @richardblackaby
Facebook: Dr Richard Blackaby.

Blackaby Ministries International (**www.blackaby.org**) is dedicated to helping people experience God. It has books and resources to assist Christians in the areas of experiencing God, spiritual leadership, revival, the marketplace, and the family. There are also resources for young adults and children. Please contact them at:

Facebook: Blackaby Ministries International
Twitter: @ExperiencingGod
Mobile App: Blackaby ministries int
Website: www.blackaby.org

Blackaby Revitalization Ministry

If you sense God wants more for your church than what you are currently experiencing, we want to help. It may well be that you have been doing everything you know to do. But that's not enough. You need to do what GOD knows you should do! You must seek Him for those answers. We can help pastors as well as church members seek a fresh word and direction from God. Let us help you experience a fresh encounter with the risen Christ so you are prepared for the great work God wants to do through your church.

Two resources that can help are the book *Flickering Lamps: Christ and His Church* and the *Flickering Lamps DVD* set. Working in conjunction with one another, these resources will help you discover God's truths for struggling, discouraged churches.

To learn more, go to **http://www.blackaby.net/revitalization/home/** or email us at **information@blackaby.org**

Blackaby Leadership Coaching

Blackaby Ministries provides coaching-based solutions to challenges faced by ministry and marketplace leaders. We also help teams achieve the focus and harmony that God intends. To learn more, go to **www.blackabycoaching.org** or email us at **information@blackaby.org**

For more information about peer coaching cohorts for pastors and ministry leaders along with information about our three day coach training workshops, visit **www.blackabycoaching.org**

Apply the truths of *Experiencing God* to every area of your church

Experiencing God: Knowing and Doing the Will of God

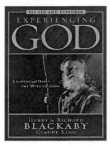

Henry Blackaby, Richard Blackaby and Claude King guide believers through seven Scriptural realities that teach us how to develop a true relationship with the Creator. By understanding how God is working through us even as we try to fathom His ways, we can begin to clearly know and do His will and discover our lives greatly and gracefully changed.

Member Book
Leader's Kit (DVDs)

Your Church Experiencing God Together

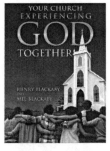

Henry and Mel Blackaby demonstrate God's plan for all believers to utilize their spiritual gifts as part of a loving church body, under Christ's headship, empowered by the Holy Spirit to become a world mission strategy center.

Member Book
DVDs

When God Speaks

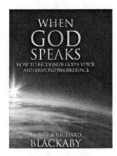

Henry and Richard Blackaby help believers to understand God does speak to His followers and that He gives clear, personal instructions that enable believers to experience fully His power, presence, and love.

Member Book

Experiencing God as Couples

Henry and Marilynn Blackaby lead married couples to experience God's presence in a way that will last a lifetime. This study has influenced thousands of lives, resulting in saved marriages, spouses coming to Jesus, rededications, couples volunteering for missions, and enriched marriages.

Member Book
DVDs

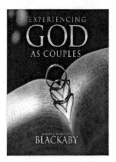

The Man God Uses: Moved from the Ordinary to the Extraordinary

Henry and Tom Blackaby provide men with a study that is designed to provide spiritual direction and encouragement. Men are being touched by God all over, and men who have encountered God need to understand what He is doing in their lives and what their lives can mean when turned over to God.

Member Book
DVDs

The Family God Uses: Becoming a Home of Influence

Tom and Kim Blackaby show parents how to discover where God is at work around their family and to learn how to join Him in that work. Use this resource to get and keep your family God-centered and teach your children their role in His kingdom.

Member Book

CPSIA information can be obtained
at www.ICGtesting.com
Printed in the USA
FSOW01n2053310717
37097FS